Milton and Music

Milton and Music is the first study to juxtapose John Milton's poetry on music with later musical adaptations of his work. In Part I: Milton on Music, Seth Herbst shows that writing about music galvanized Milton's intellectual development towards animist materialism, the belief that everything in the universe—even the human soul—is made of matter. The Milton who emerges is a forward-thinking visionary who leaped past his contemporaries in conceiving music as a material phenomenon that exists simultaneously as sound and metaphor. Part II: Milton in Music follows two daring composers in investigating whether Milton's visionary concept of music can be realized in actual musical sound. In *Samson*, an oratorio adaptation of Milton's *Samson Agonistes*, Handel resists Miltonic music theory, suggesting that music struggles to function as both sound and metaphor. By contrast, the twentieth-century Polish composer Krzysztof Penderecki composes an iconoclastic opera of *Paradise Lost* that develops a soundworld of fractured dissonance in which music acts as both sound and metaphor. Recovering Milton's own high estimation of music from a critical tradition that has subordinated it to the poet's political and religious convictions, Herbst reveals Milton as an interdisciplinary thinker and overlooked figure in the study of words and music. Driven by bold claims about the comparative treatment of literature and music, *Milton and Music* revises our understanding of what makes this canonical poet an intellectual revolutionary.

Seth Herbst studies the relation between poetry and music in Milton and Shakespeare and later musical adaptations of their work. Herbst was trained in literature and music at Harvard, where he received an undergraduate degree in both disciplines and a PhD in early modern literature. Formerly a freelance music critic for *The Boston Globe*, Herbst is assistant professor of English at the United States Military Academy.

Routledge Focus on Literature

Speech Acts in Blake's *Milton*
Brian Russell Graham

Literature, Education, and Society
Bridging the Gap
Charles F. Altieri

Shakespeare and the Theater of Pity
Shawn Smith

Trauma, Memory and Silence of the Irish Woman in Contemporary Literature
Wounds of the Body and the Soul
Edited by Madalina Armie and Verónica Membrive

Rilke's Hands
An Essay on Gentleness
Harold Schweizer

Orality, Form, and Lyric Unity
Poetics of Michael Donaghy and Don Paterson
Beverley Nadin

Milton and Music
Seth Herbst

For more information about this series, please visit: www.routledge.com/Routledge-Focus-on-Literature/book-series/RFLT

Milton and Music

Seth Herbst

NEW YORK AND LONDON

First published 2023
by Routledge
605 Third Avenue, New York, NY 10158

and by Routledge
4 Park Square, Milton Park, Abingdon, Oxon, OX14 4RN

Routledge is an imprint of the Taylor & Francis Group, an informa business

© 2023 Seth Herbst

The right of Seth Herbst to be identified as author of this work has been asserted in accordance with sections 77 and 78 of the Copyright, Designs and Patents Act 1988.

All rights reserved. No part of this book may be reprinted or reproduced or utilised in any form or by any electronic, mechanical, or other means, now known or hereafter invented, including photocopying and recording, or in any information storage or retrieval system, without permission in writing from the publishers.

Trademark notice: Product or corporate names may be trademarks or registered trademarks, and are used only for identification and explanation without intent to infringe.

ISBN: 978-1-032-45721-5 (hbk)
ISBN: 978-1-032-45722-2 (pbk)
ISBN: 978-1-003-37838-9 (ebk)

DOI: 10.4324/9781003378389

Typeset in Times New Roman
by Newgen Publishing UK

In memory of Daniel Albright, David Elliott, and Barbara Lewalski

Contents

Acknowledgements	viii
Introduction	1
PART I **Milton on Music**	15
1 Music as Matter	17
2 "Pure Concent": Music as Sound and Metaphor	38
PART II **Milton in Music**	65
3 Handel's Cacophony: *Samson*, Noise, and the Right to Music	67
4 Making a Hell of Heaven and Earth: Music as Sound and Metaphor in Penderecki's *Paradise Lost*	91
Conclusion	115
Works Cited and Consulted	129
Index	136

Acknowledgements

Barbara Lewalski encouraged me to write about Milton and music; Stephen Greenblatt, Gordon Teskey, and Leah Whittington urged me to dig deeper. Dan Albright ushered me into the world of words and music; Helen Vendler talked me through the final stages of this book. David Elliott, the voice of Harvard Radio and my dear friend, believed in me. Elizabeth D. Samet has guided me as a teacher and author. Heather Souvaine Horn read the final manuscript with the inspired eye of a master editor and writer. I owe more than I can say to friends and mentors: Kathy Gerlach, David A. Harper, Adam Keller, Elizabeth Lazzari, David Nee, Joshua Roling, Richard Schoonhoven, Misha Teramura, and Anthony Zupancic. I am grateful to my parents, Eric and Judy; to my sisters and their families—Elisabeth, Emmanuel, Julia, Gabriel, and Margo; Andrea, Jacques, Charlotte, and Isabelle; and above all, to my brilliant wife, Saori, and my kingly son, Solomon.

An earlier version of Chapter 1 appeared as "Sound as Matter: Milton, Music, and Monism" in *Milton, Materialism, and Embodiment: One First Matter All* (Duquesne UP / Penn St. UP, 2017), reprinted by kind permission of Penn State University Press. Chapter 2 and part of the Introduction appeared in an earlier version as "Milton and Music," *Essays in Criticism* 66.1, reprinted by kind permission of Oxford University Press. I am grateful to Caroline Kane for her kind assistance with permissions for Penderecki's *Paradise Lost*:

Krzysztof Penderecki PARADISE LOST
Libretto by Christopher Fry
Original text by John Milton
Copyright © 1978 by Schott Music GmbH & Co. KG, Mainz, Germany
All Rights Reserved
Used by arrangement with European American Music Distributors Company, sole US and Canadian agent for Schott Music GmbH & Co. KG, Mainz, Germany.

Introduction

This book presents a new interdisciplinary approach to exploring the relation between John Milton and music. No previous monograph has paired Milton's own extensive poetic representations of music with later musical adaptations of his work. *Milton and Music* does just that. In Part I: Milton on Music, I offer a fresh reading of Milton's thinking about music; then, in Part II: Milton in Music, I offer readings of notable musical adaptations that shed new light on Milton's poetry.

This interdisciplinary approach offers a timely intervention in a field that is, paradoxically, both emerging and established. While Milton's intense interest in music has long been recognized, the topic has, oddly, remained peripheral for scholars.[1] Yet over the past decade, several literary scholars have begun to develop new ways of studying Milton and music. My interdisciplinary method is attuned to Milton's own background as both a poet and a passionate amateur musician, and this book reveals Milton himself as an interdisciplinary thinker. Yet until very recently, the scant literary scholarship on music as a theme in Milton's poetry has tended to underplay the poet's high regard for this sibling art.

More work has been done at the length of the essay than of the monograph. An older strand of criticism, active in the 1970s through the early 1990s, situated Milton within the musical milieu of his day. Critics in this tradition tended to produce historicist essays focused on individual lyric poems or works of prose, rather than embracing the larger vision of Milton's body of poetry on music.[2] A newer strand of criticism, meanwhile, has tended to elevate other concerns—theology, politics, poetics, or science—over Milton's treatment of music itself. This critical work has had the curious effect of de-emphasizing the crucial importance music itself plays in Milton's imagination.

Several recent critics understand the music described in Milton's poetry as a metaphor for politics, for cosmological order, or for poetry

DOI: 10.4324/9781003378389-1

itself. Marc Berley and Andrew Mattison locate Milton's interest in music in its capacity to stand in as a metaphor for poetry. Mattison goes so far as to classify Milton's various accounts of music in the 1645 *Poems* as a coded "defense of poetry" (Mattison 622).[3] These accounts downplay Milton's sensory engagement in the acoustic properties of music, and more significantly, as I will argue, fail to capture how the attempt to describe music fueled Milton's intellectual development. In the few instances in which the music in Milton's poetry has been considered on its own terms, scholars have generally agreed that Milton classifies it as an inferior sister to poetry. Stephen Buhler, who is willing to treat music as a literal event in Milton's poetry, argues that Milton's concern for language outweighs his respect for music.[4]

More recent criticism has pointed in exciting new directions. Katherine Larson provides a welcome focus on music itself, engaging with early modern performance practice to reveal song in Milton as a performance of "affective power" by an embodied and gendered singer (Larson 106).[5] Katherine Cox attends to early modern acoustical science in an imaginative account of "satanic acoustics" in *Paradise Lost* that reveals how Milton's depiction of Satan and his crew of fallen angels is informed by imagery of musical instrumentation.[6] Still, there is more critical work to be done, I think, with the accounts of music in Milton's poetry.

Only over the last decade have scholarly monographs about Milton and music appeared. The first, Erin Minear's *Reverberating Song in Shakespeare and Milton: Language, Memory, and Musical Representation* (Ashgate, 2011), offers a comprehensive account of Milton's writings on music. Yet over half of the book is devoted to Shakespeare. Minear's conclusion "describes Milton's final rejection of Shakespearean music, his ultimate association of delightful sounds with falseness and playacting" (Minear 16).[7] I hold, to the contrary, that Milton never loses his high regard for music.

The only book solely on Milton and music currently in print is David Ainsworth's recent *Milton, Music and Literary Interpretation: Reading Through the Spirit* (Routledge, 2020). Ainsworth, like Minear, is not focused exclusively on the topic of music itself.[8] Ainsworth aims to relate music to theology, developing a stimulating account of pneumatology, the theology of the Holy Spirit. Like Cox's, Ainsworth's work usefully expands the scope of Milton and music studies. Yet while I, too, am interested in how Milton connects music with the principles of his Christian faith, I remain more interested in questions of explicit representation of music in Milton's poetry.[9]

On the other hand, it is possible to exaggerate the degree to which Milton's poetry is indebted to music. Diane McColley's wide-ranging monograph, *Poetry and Music in Seventeenth-Century England* (Cambridge UP, 1997), gives a rich snapshot of the seventeenth-century musical scene and valuably places Milton in the literary context of Donne and Herbert. But while McColley offers some rewarding insights, her discussion is hampered by the contention that Milton's verse itself is "musical," a claim she attempts to substantiate by applying musical terms of analysis to poetry.[10] To the contrary, I find that Milton generally avoids mimetic simulations of musical form or harmony.

I undertake to achieve a sense of Milton as a musically informed poet whose extensive writing about music has not yet been fully appreciated as a unified body of thought. I also add a new focus—new, that is, with respect to studies of Milton and music—on later musical adaptations of Milton's work. The book is divided into two complementary halves. In the first part, "Milton on Music," I consider the poet's engagement with music, which I argue influences his intellectual development in ways that have yet to be recognized. Restoring a critical sense of Milton's own high regard for music, I contend that the poet understands music—not poetry—as the highest artistic medium in God's universe. Writing about music consequently drives Milton towards some of his most distinctive philosophical and poetic positions. In the book's second part, "Milton in Music," I explore the poet's "afterlife" in musical adaptations of his works, the study of which yields new insights both into Milton and into the composers who rose to the challenge of adapting his poetry into music. Ultimately, Milton emerges as a visionary interdisciplinary thinker whose demanding conception of music both provokes and confounds musical adaptation.[11] Music in Milton's own time inspired the poet's thinking but may not have lived up to the aesthetic and ethical ideals he conferred on it in his poetry. Only in the twentieth century, enfranchised by the dissonance of modernist and postmodernist musical harmony, does it seem music can fully catch up to Milton's poetic vision of it.

Part I: Milton on Music

What is it about music that stimulates Milton's imagination? In the 1644 prose tract "Of Education," Milton proposes that music can help students at his ideal school balance intellectual and physical demands:

> The interim of unsweating themselves regularly, and convenient rest before meat may both with profit and delight be taken up in

recreating and composing their travail'd spirits with the solemn and divine harmonies of musick heard or learnt; either while the skilful *Organist* plies his grave and fancied descant, in lofty fugues, or the whole Symphony with artfull and unimaginable touches adorn and grace the well studied chords of some choise Composer; sometimes the Lute, or soft organ stop waiting on elegant voices either to Religious, martiall, or civill ditties; which if wise men & Prophets be not extreamly out, have a great power over dispositions and manners, to smooth and make them gentle from rustick harshness and distemper'd passions. The like also would not be unexpedient after meat to assist and cherish nature in her first concoction,[12] and send their mindes back to study in good tune and satisfaction.

(Milton, *CPW* II 409–11)[13]

On Milton's account, listening to music has a beneficial psychosomatic effect, relaxing the body and soothing the mind (or digestive tract). This seems little more than a stock borrowing from Platonic theory not uncommon in Renaissance writing about music; specific types of music, early modern thinkers recalled from *The Republic*, induce specific effects on listeners, and music should be deployed, Plato argues, so as to encourage admirable qualities and discourage unworthy qualities.[14] But there is more here than Plato. For Milton, music seems to have a mysterious power to raise the condition of fallen human beings.

What precisely is this power, and wherein does it lie? Something is at work behind the passage from "Of Education," a set of assumptions about music that Milton does not fully articulate but that nonetheless undergirds his argument and makes possible the particular efficacy he claims for music. We can begin to infer some of those assumptions by noting that Milton describes music in two separate dimensions: formal aesthetic qualities and effects on the listener. In the first dimension, Milton notes that music has an abstract or mathematical form, *harmony*, which is then realized in sound as a particular texture, according to varying performing forces and compositional styles. As for the second dimension, the effect of music on listeners, Milton is concerned not so much with Plato's taxonomic classification, in which different kinds of music induce different effects, but rather with the way in which music can serve simultaneously to ameliorate the condition of both body and spirit.

Indeed, for Milton music seems to elide the perception of body and spirit as disjunct entities. As bodies "unsweat themselves" or as they work to concoct ingested food, music aids these physiological processes—even as it acts simultaneously to compose or calm wearied spirits, and to prepare the mind to return to study. This is not just a simultaneity of action. There is a sense that music causes body and mind to intertwine. In the most influential account of Milton's monist materialism, *Milton Among the Philosophers*, Stephen Fallon cites this passage as evidence that Milton had begun to think of the soul as a corporeal phenomenon. Fallon argues that Milton's punning language—"*composing* their travaill'd spirits," "send their minds back to study *in good tune*" (emphasis added)—glances at the materialist philosophy the poet would later develop more fully in his divorce tracts, in *De Doctrina Christiana*, and in *Paradise Lost*. "Like Bacon," Fallon declares regarding "Of Education," "Milton follows Plato and Aristotle on the effects of music but suggests that the medium of the effect is corporeal motion" (Fallon 89). In other words, Milton's musical puns imply that since students' "spirits" and "mind" can be shaped and tuned like a musical composition, those spirits and mind can be understood as material phenomena. For Fallon, the crucial point is that Milton implies the corporeality of the soul. Of equal interest, I will argue in my first chapter, is the question of why—and how—it is *music* that makes the soul seem corporeal. It is striking that even when writing "Of Education" in 1644, when he has yet to formulate the body and soul explicitly as a single, continuous entity, Milton still allows music to knit body and soul together in a moment of heightened, holistic perception. The power of music to knit body and soul is the primary topic of my first chapter, which argues that music, for Milton, is itself a material phenomenon. How distinctive is Milton in this view? While some other early modern thinkers also understood music in material terms, they tended to worry that this materiality had a suspect influence on the human soul. Music posed a problem, a challenge to the separation between body and soul. For Milton, however, this challenge is precisely what leads towards his radical monist materialism: the material nature of music helps to reveal the material nature of the soul.

Music stimulates Milton intellectually, then, because it offers him an aesthetic tie between the physiological and the spiritual, raising the fallen human—if briefly and incompletely—by unifying our disjunct perception of body and soul. But this insight does not address wherein, precisely, music's power lies. Indeed, there seems to be a missing link in Milton's representation of music as I have described it: an explanation for why music, as an aesthetic form, induces such an effect on listeners. What allows music to merge the listener's perception of body and soul? The answer to that question, it turns out, is found not in "Of Education" but somewhat earlier in Milton's career, and not in prose, but in poetry.

Milton's first published volume of poetry, the 1645 *Poems*, offers many passages on music, but only a single, seemingly unassuming lyric is exclusively devoted to the topic. This lyric, "At a Solemn Music," offers a fully realized, comprehensive poetic model of music. As I demonstrate, Milton's model holds that music is at once an acoustic phenomenon but also, at the same time, a metaphor representing the relation between God and his creatures. Simultaneously acoustic phenomenon and metaphor, music offers Milton an aesthetic analogy with the monist theological concept of the unified body and soul. This analogy explains music's capacity, for Milton, to knit together the listener's perception of body and soul. It is worth noting, however, that this sense of the listener's experience is necessarily theoretical; Milton is, of course, writing poetry *about* music rather than, like his composer father, writing actual music. In Part II of this book, I will take up the question of whether real music, as actually composed, can present itself as both acoustic phenomenon and metaphor.[15]

The model of music as both acoustic and metaphorical drives an important strand of Milton's larger thinking about the Christian experience: the tension between beauty and morality. This strand—a perennial Christian concern but of peculiar interest for Milton—is the central topic of my second chapter. In its simultaneity of acoustics and metaphor, the model of music staked out in "At a Solemn Music" provides Milton with a vehicle for reconciling moral duty with sensuous beauty, ethics with aesthetics. Music stands as the keystone of the poet's extraordinary effort, in *Paradise Lost*, to make Christian obedience the ultimate aesthetic and moral experience. After first laying out Milton's model of music as the poet delineates it in "At a Solemn Music," I proceed to explore how Milton employs it in *Paradise Lost*, in the Ludlow *Masque*, and, most radically, in *Samson Agonistes*. Together with the Nativity Ode, these are the central texts for the first two chapters; they constitute what I take to be the nerve center of Milton's poetic account of music.[16]

The first two chapters thus offer an inquiry into Milton's theoretical account of music. This first part of the book represents my conviction that Milton's poetic account of music is central to his intellectual development and to his core beliefs about the role of art in human experience. It also points towards the second part of the book, where I turn to later musical adaptations of Milton's works. My purpose in doing so is both to explore what sort of music Milton's complex poetry provokes and to investigate whether actual music can realize—or at least simulate—the theoretical properties Milton ascribes to it.

Part II: Milton in Music

The second half of the book adopts an interdisciplinary mode of analysis by presenting readings of two notable musical adaptations of Milton's works. The study of the adaptation of art—including translation from one language into another as well as from one medium into another—is a flourishing scholarly enterprise, practiced across disciplines from film studies to art history to musicology. As far as literature and music are concerned, the closest precedent for studying musical adaptations of Milton lies in Shakespeare studies. The adaptation of Shakespeare into music has generated a diverse body of scholarship.[17] Yet Milton scholarship has yet to follow suit.[18] One principal reason is that, unlike Shakespeare, Milton has been infrequently adapted into music. A mere handful of musical works based on Milton's poetry exists; some of these works, like Haydn's *Creation*, are based only loosely on Milton.[19] Is it, then, worthwhile to study musical adaptations of Milton? The relatively few composers who have taken on Milton have not done so lightly. They and their librettists—those important yet often unsung figures who draft the text for a musical drama—must grapple not only with the particular stylistic and representational challenges presented by Milton's complex, difficult poetry, but also the specter of Milton's own thinking about music, threaded as it is through his poetry. As a result, the musical adaptations of Milton that composers have produced tend to stand out as high points within their compositional output. Furthermore, and more importantly for my purposes here, in their efforts to render Milton's poetry in fitting music, these composers shed new light on Milton's originals—and Milton's own dynamic thinking about music.

Yet one might well object to my method in conjoining "Milton on music" with "Milton in music." Beyond the bridging of literary studies and musicology, which is no longer an uncommon approach, one might further object that in taking up musical adaptations from the eighteenth and twentieth centuries, the book also rides roughshod over disjunct historical periods. This disjunction, I suggest, is not a problem but rather a rich opportunity. To attend to later musical adaptations of Milton is to engage in a mode of reception history, which has become one of the dominant concerns of Milton studies. Driven in large part by resurgent interest in book history, the study of Milton's reception history has recently experienced something like a revolution.[20] Yet while that revolution has embraced the material world of the text, it has yet to concentrate on music as a medium of artistic response. This book aims to bring the musical reception of Milton into the mainstream as an important avenue of inquiry in reception history.

In chapters 3 and 4, I turn to two seminal works by two prominent composers of different periods who are attracted to contrasting elements of Milton's imagination. The third chapter takes up Handel's adaptation of Milton's closet drama, *Samson Agonistes*. Handel's oratorio, titled simply *Samson* (1742), might seem at first blush a mismatch of composer and literary source. Handel's compositional idiom, with its regal grandeur and effortless refinement, may not strike one as ideally suited to realizing the anguished intensity and metrically experimental poetry of Milton's late style. But we can learn a great deal about what makes Milton's drama distinctive as we track how Handel reimagines the sparsely peopled closet drama as a bustling Baroque oratorio. Most of all, as Handel confronts the challenge of rendering in music the offstage noise of Samson's destruction of the temple, we see how the composer grapples with the same formal challenge that confronted Milton when he wrote the climax of his closet drama: how to render cacophony—that relentless assault on aesthetic order—within the formal framework of art. As I show in Part I, Milton daringly incorporates cacophony into his theory of musical sound. In Handel's eighteenth-century musical practice, however, cacophony represents something like the undoing of music itself. Ultimately, Handel is understandably less audacious than Milton, ingeniously evading the problem of cacophony by rendering it in purely symbolic, rather than expressively acoustic, terms. In other words, Handel does not dare to make his music actually sound like cacophony. In so doing, Handel challenges Milton's theory of music as both sound and metaphor, suggesting that the poet's concept of music is richer, or at least has more expressive potential, than actual music itself.

My final chapter, however, takes up a composer who successfully enacts Milton's own theoretical ideals for music. Krzysztof Penderecki (1933–2020), a twentieth-century Polish composer among the most prominent voices in classical music after World War II, composed a large-scale opera based on *Paradise Lost*. Unlike Handel, of course, Penderecki is enfranchised by the dissonance of post-tonal twentieth-century harmony. Yet a musical idiom admitting dissonance does not itself guarantee a compelling realization of Milton's musical theory into actual music. But Penderecki does indeed manage the feat. In a measure of his own distinctive identity as a composer, Penderecki matches Milton's effort to reconcile the aesthetic and ethical dimensions of music.

Like Milton, Penderecki focuses on the role music can play in negotiating the unremitting anguish of the postlapsarian human condition.

Writing after the savage destructiveness of two world wars, Penderecki forged a complex and challenging style to capture the condition of fallenness in human experience. Despite—or perhaps because of—his vast stylistic distance from what Milton himself would have understood as music, Penderecki offers a profound realization of Milton's theoretical claim that music is at once metaphor and acoustical object. In his opera—which the composer classifies, after a genre of Renaissance sacred music, as *Sacra Rappresentazione*—Penderecki constructs a musical soundworld that at once expressively evokes the anguish of fallenness but also stands as a metaphor for fallenness itself. A bleaker vision of the human fall than Milton's own, Penderecki's opera is the closest any musical adaptation of Milton has yet come to realizing both the epic scale of *Paradise Lost* but also the nuanced musical theory that, as I show in Part I, drives Milton's intellectual development.

Written in 1975–78 as a commission for the Lyric Opera of Chicago, Penderecki's work was debuted in 1978 to a mostly indifferent critical response.[21] It has been performed only a handful of times since. The reasons for this neglect are at once easy to see and hard to understand. This is challenging music, for both performers and audience, and it is a setting of a religious epic poem that is, unlike the dramas of Shakespeare, no longer at the forefront of secular public consciousness. Yet Penderecki is scarcely a minor composer, and many of his frequently performed works—especially works composed prior to *Paradise Lost*, such as the famous *Threnody for the Victims of Hiroshima* (1960)—are at least as challenging as this opera. It is high time that Penderecki's *Paradise Lost* be recognized as a milestone of twentieth-century opera and a powerful response to Milton's epic vision. In my final chapter, I hope to direct attention back to an overlooked musical masterpiece and, in demonstrating Penderecki's successful realization of Milton's own musical theory, to point back to how Milton himself understands music in a visionary but practical way that prior studies of him have tended to obscure.

The subject of Milton and music remains rich with possibility. The young Milton grew up in a musical household, and there is biographical evidence that his youthful passion for music only deepened over the years.[22] The present book is not, however, concerned with the well-trod ground of biography. Instead, what I explore here are the ways in which thinking and writing about music stimulated Milton towards some of his most characteristically radical intellectual and aesthetic positions, and the ways in which Milton, in turn, impelled musical composers to create some of their most characteristic and challenging works. It is my hope that this book will diversify the burgeoning interest in Milton and music into a genuine partnership between literary and musical analysis, expanding our understanding of Milton's engagement with music and highlighting the study of musical adaptation of Milton's poetry as an untapped source for critical reception history.

Notes

1 John Milton senior was a respected amateur composer, and John Milton junior grew up hearing and performing music. There are various traces of Milton junior's lifelong engagement with music. For an account of Milton's musical milieu, see John Harper, "'One Equal Music': The Music of Milton's Youth," *Milton Quarterly* 31.1 (Mar. 1997), 1–10.
2 See, for instance, James D. Brophy, "Milton's 'Warble': The Trill as Metaphor of Concord," *Milton Quarterly* 19.4 (Dec. 1985), 105–109; Nan Cooke Carpenter, "Milton and Music: Henry Lawes, Dante, and Casella," *English Literary Renaissance* 2.2 (Spring 1972), 237–242; Audrey Davidson, "Milton on the Music of Henry Lawes," *Milton Newsletter* 2.2 (May 1968), 19–23; M. N. K. Mander, "The *Epistola ad Patrem*: Milton's Apology for Poetry," *Milton Quarterly* 23.4 (Dec. 1989), 158–66, as well as "Milton and the Music of the Spheres," *Milton Quarterly* 24.2 (May 1990), 63–71, and "Music in Milton's *Hymn*," *Renaissance Studies* 5.4 (Dec. 1991), 412–426; Harinder S. Marjara, "Milton's 'Chromatick jarres' and 'Tuscan Aire,'" *Milton Quarterly* 19.1 (Mar. 1985), 11–13. Somewhat more recent is Mary Elizabeth Basile's analysis of the surviving music from the Ludlow *Masque*, "The Music of *A Maske*," *Milton Quarterly* 27.3 (Oct. 1993), 85–98.
3 See Andrew Mattison, "Sweet Imperfection: Milton and the Troubled Metaphor of Harmony," *Modern Philology* 106.4 (May 2009), 617–647, esp. p. 618; and Marc Berley, "Introduction" and "Milton's Earthly Grossness: Music and the Condition of the Poet," in *After the Heavenly Tune: English Poetry and the Aspiration to Song* (Pittsburgh, PA: Duquesne UP, 2000), 1–26, 141–205.
4 See Stephen M. Buhler, "Counterpoint and Controversy: Milton and the Critiques of Polyphonic Music," *Milton Studies* 36 (1998), 18–40. Buhler's primary concern is to locate Milton within the seventeenth-century debate on the place of polyphony in liturgical music. Buhler's analysis in some ways belongs more to the older tradition of exploring Milton's relation to his musical milieu.
5 See Katherine R. Larson, "'Blest pair of *Sirens*... Voice and Verse': Milton's Rhetoric of Song," *Milton Studies* 54 (2013), 81–106, as well as "Sweet Echo," in *The Matter of Song in Early Modern England* (Oxford, Oxford UP, 2019), 179–202.
6 See Katherine Cox, "'How cam'st thou speakable of mute': Satanic Acoustics in *Paradise Lost*," *Milton Studies* 57 (2016), 233–260.
7 See Erin Minear, *Reverberating Song in Shakespeare and Milton: Language, Memory, and Musical Representation* (Burlington, VT: Ashgate, 2011,

reprinted New York, NY: Routledge, 2016). While Minear is interested in a different set of concerns than I am in this book, hers is a powerful study that will continue to shape our understanding of music in Shakespeare and Milton.

8 Ainsworth laid the groundwork for his book in an earlier essay, "Rapturous Milton and the Communal Harmony of Faith," *Milton Quarterly* 47.3 (2013), 149–162. Ainsworth understands music in Milton primarily as a metaphor for Christian community. Ainsworth takes up many of the same passages I consider and offers some analytic terms close to my own, but Ainsworth is concerned with how music promotes Christian community, where I am concerned with how music allows Milton to balance between aesthetics and ethics. Ainsworth's book clarifies further the distinction between his work and mine.

9 See Ainsworth, *Milton, Music and Literary Interpretation: Reading through the Spirit* (New York: Routledge, 2020), especially chapter 4, "Harmonious Reading," 94–119.

10 See Diane Kelsey McColley, "'Sole, or responsive': voices in Milton's choirs," in *Poetry and Music in Seventeenth-Century England* (Cambridge, UK: Cambridge UP, 1997), 175–217.

11 For suggesting the use of the word "provoke" in this context, I am grateful to Susan Lintelmann, Manuscripts Curator in the Special Collections Division of the United States Military Academy Library.

12 The *OED* states: "The old physiology recognized three processes: *first concoction*, digestion in the stomach and intestines; *second concoction*, the process whereby the chyme so formed is changed into blood; *third concoction*, secretion" ("concoction, *n*.1.b.").

13 For citations from the Yale *Complete Prose Works of John Milton*, I abbreviate the source as *CPW*; the roman numeral refers to the volume.

14 This Platonic strand of thought was still current in Milton's day. See, for instance, Thomas Wright's discussion of music in *The Passions of the Mind* (London, 1601, revised 1604): "As musicke and instruments in one kind causeth soldiers blood to rise, and thirst after the shedding of the blood of their enemies: so contrariwise another sort of musicke pacifieth the minds of men, and rendreth them quiet and peaceable" (166–67). Wright explicitly acknowledges the classical origins of his account of music, though he mistakes Plato for Aristotle: "*Aristotle* in his common-wealth forbiddeth a certaine sort of lascivious musicke, and alloweth the Doricall" (165). I quote from the 1604 revised text of *Passions of the Mind*, lightly modernizing orthography.

15 I am grateful to David Ainsworth, in reviewing my manuscript, for suggesting that Milton's thinking about music is theoretical and can be both linked to and contrasted with actual music as I examine it in the second half of the book.

16 Milton does write about music in other poems: *L'Allegro* and *Il Penseroso, Ad Patrem*, the three poems inspired by Leonora Baroni, and the commendatory sonnet to Henry Lawes. In prose, Milton also takes up the subject

of music in the second prolusion, "On the Music of the Spheres." While these accounts of music are richly detailed and the second prolusion reveals a precocious engagement with music as a system for thinking about the cosmos, they are on the whole more aesthetically and intellectually conventional than Milton's daringly imaginative representation of music in my core texts. For a reading of music in *L'Allegro*, juxtaposed with George Frideric Handel's musical adaptation of it, see the conclusion to this book.

17 Shakespeare and music criticism is too ample to summarize here. For a useful general collection, see *Shakespeare, Music and Performance*, edited by Bill Barclay and David Lindley (Cambridge: Cambridge UP, 2017). For a more individual approach, see Daniel Albright, *Musicking Shakespeare: A Conflict of Theatres* (Rochester, NY: U Rochester P, 2007). My own interdisciplinary approach in the present book is in part inspired by Albright's.

18 There are few essays by literary scholars on musical adaptations of Milton's works. What little there is tends to be informational or reviews. See, for example, Stella P. Revard, "Handel's *Samson:* London, 1985," *Milton Quarterly* 21.1 (Mar. 1987), 28–30; Paul G. Stanwood, "'Paradise Lost': Epic and Opera," *Early Modern Literary Studies* 15.3 (Jan. 2011). Scholarship on these works tends to originate in other disciplines. For instance, see Rachel Duerden, "The Mis-shapen Pearl: Morris, Handel, Milton, and *L'Allegro, il Penseroso ed il Moderato*," *Dance Research* 28.2 (Nov. 2010), 200–217; or Michael O'Connell and John Powell, "Music and Sense in Handel's Setting of Milton's *L'Allegro* and *Il Penseroso*," *Eighteenth-Century Studies* 12.1 (Autumn 1978), 16–46. The musicologist Ruth Smith has written on Handel's Milton adaptations. See Smith, "Milton Modulated for Handel's Music," in *Milton in the Long Restoration*, edited by Blair Hoxby and Ann Baynes Coiro (Oxford, UK: Oxford UP, 2016), 159–177. One of the few genuine attempts to write about musical adaptation is Stephen Buhler's "'Soft *Lydian* Airs' Meet 'Anthems clear': Intelligibility in Milton, Handel, and Mark Morris," *John Donne Journal* 25 (2006), 333–353.

19 For a survey of some of the byways of the repertoire, as well as some observations on Handel and Haydn, see Brian Morris, "'Not Without Song': Milton and the Composers," in *Approaches to* Paradise Lost, ed. C.A. Patrides (London, 1968), 137–61.

20 John Leonard's two-volume reception history, *Faithful Labourers* (2013), sums up the critical tradition and points the way forward for reception history. A pathbreaking work of recent scholarship is David A. Harper's "The First Annotator of *Paradise Lost* and the Makings of English Literary Criticism," *SEL 1500–1900* 59.3 (Summer 2019), 507–530, which argues that "P.H.," the first annotator of *Paradise Lost* (1695), has been misidentified as the Scottish Patrick Hume; the real author, Harper contends, was Peter Hume, "a Nonconformist servant in the [Restoration] Royal Household" (Harper 520). Harper draws bold conclusions about this first critical edition of *Paradise Lost* as a watershed moment in the development of literary criticism.

Introduction   13

21   One theme of reviews was that Penderecki was less boldly unconventional in *Paradise Lost* than in his earlier works. See, for example, Linda Marie Delloff, "A Fall from Grace," *Christian Century* 96.2 (Jan. 17, 1979), 52–54, or Art Lange, "Penderecki's 'Paradise Lost,'" *Tempo* New Series No. 128 (Mar. 1979), 34–35: "The composer appears to have been somewhat intimidated by the gravity of the subject matter" (Lange 34). In *Newsweek* (Dec. 11, 1978), Hubert Saal was savage: "Last week, at a cost of nearly $1 million and after a delay of two years, 'Paradise Lost' was finally unveiled in Chicago. It turned out to be a fool's paradise. Lasting more than three hours, it packed the dramatic wallop of a grounded blimp. The Puritan in Milton would have applauded Penderecki's score for its unrelieved dissonance and funeral pace" (Saal 90). Andrew Porter, writing in *The New Yorker* (Dec. 18, 1978), was more perceptive: "there is a bold attempt, unmatched in any of the earlier 'Paradise Lost' reworkings I know, to present things on the Miltonic scale" (Porter 88). But Porter, too, sides with the prosecution, noting the "inadequacy of Fry's text [i.e., the libretto] and, even more, of Penderecki's own music—in weight, sounds, rhythms, and syntax—to deal with the tremendous subject" (Porter 90).

22   See John Harper, "'One Equal Music': The Music of Milton's Youth," *Milton Quarterly* 31.1 (Mar. 1997), 1–10.

Part I
Milton on Music

1 Music as Matter

In the vibrant universe of *Paradise Lost*, everything that exists has a material form, fashioned from the substance of God's body.[1] What about music? It may be produced by matter—by the throat and lungs, by musical instruments—but once released into the air, can music really act and feel like matter? It is a central part of my argument in this chapter that Milton does indeed make music in *Paradise Lost* a material phenomenon.

Milton's representation of music in *Paradise Lost* is radical. But its materiality alone is not what makes it so. While the notion that an early modern thinker could construe music as matter might well strike the twenty-first-century observer as surprising, it was in fact not uncommon to understand music as a material phenomenon. As Gina Bloom and other scholars have shown, a material conception of sound—sound as produced by matter, transmitted through matter, and received via the material organ of the ear—emerges in key texts of early modern literature and theology.[2] That Milton would represent music as material in his epic is itself, then, not altogether remarkable in the context of early modern thought.

But the early modern materialist understanding of sound was not uncontested or uncontroversial. For one, it threatened the ancient but still attractive Pythagorean sense of music as a conceptual model for the structure of cosmos, the so-called "harmony of the spheres." If music were simply a physical phenomenon, could it still be a paradigm for the construction of the universe?[3] A more dangerous debate involved larger anxieties about the effect of the material world on the soul. If music were matter, what did it mean for musical sound to exert such a palpable influence on the human spirit? In *The Passions of the Mind* (1601, revised 1604), Thomas Wright articulates the problem succinctly:

DOI: 10.4324/9781003378389-3

> How [is it that] musicke stirreth up these passions, and moveth so mightily these affections? What hath the shaking or artificiall crispling of the aire (which is in effect the substance of musicke) to doe with rousing up choler, afflicting with melancholie, jubilating the heart with pleasure, elevating the soul with devotion, alluring to lust, inducing to peace, exciting to passion, inviting to magnanimitie?
>
> (168)

For Wright, the answer to the question of how music stirs up our passions would seem to lie in a mysterious affinity between musical sound and the soul, what Wright calls "a certaine sympathie, correspondence, or proportion betwixt our soules and musicke" (168). "So we may say," Wright proposes, "that such is the nature of our soules, as musicke hath a certaine proportionat sympathie with them: as our tasts have with such varieties of dantie cates, our smelling such varietie of odurs, &c." (168). Yet this mysterious sympathy, explicable only by analogy with the senses of taste or smell, strikes Wright as insufficient to explain "this miracle in nature" (168). The deeper explanation might lie in the ultimate mystery:

> The second manner of this miracle in nature [i.e., the effect of music on the soul], some assign and ascribe to Gods generall providence, who when these sounds affect the eare, produceth a certaine spirituall qualitie in the soule, the which stirreth up one or other passion, according to the varietie of voices, or conforts of instruments.
>
> (168)

God steps in to perform the miracle, carrying musical effects into the human soul. Undergirding this account is a firm dualism, a distinction between physical matter and the human soul. The key point, for Wright, is that music in physical terms cannot itself affect the immaterial soul. This is why God must step in: "So corporall musicke being unable to worke such extraordinarie effects in our soules, God by his ordinarie natural providence produceth them [i.e., musical effects on the soul]" (168). Yet even this explanation does not satisfy Wright, perhaps because it hints at a kind of materialist monism, suggesting a physical dimension in which the soul can receive musical effects from God. Finally, for Wright, an evasion is necessary. Music is indeed material, and it produces an extraordinary effect on human emotions, but this effect occurs not in the soul, but rather in the "heart":

the very sound itselfe, which according to the best philosophie, is nothing else but a certaine artificiall shaking, crispling, or tickling of the ayre [...] passeth thorow the eares, and by them unto the heart, and there beateth and tickleth it in such sort, as it is moved with semblable [i.e., corresponding] passions.

(170)

This convenient relegation of emotion to the physical heart, an organ removed from the immaterial soul, allows Wright to rescue the soul as a separate entity from the body. Ultimately, then, for Wright, music confirms a nuanced but rigid dualism in which music pertains to the physical world while the soul remains an immaterial thing apart, subject only to the direct manipulation of God.[4]

What distinguishes Milton from this representative early modern way of thinking about music and the human soul is how he combines a materialist understanding of music with a materialist understanding of the human soul.

Milton's distinctive brand of materialism, most often termed monist or animist materialism, has been of outstanding interest to Miltonists over the past few decades. How did Milton arrive at such a radical theological position? In what has been accepted as the standard account of the poet's intellectual development, Stephen Fallon argues that Milton's monist materialism developed gradually over the course of his life. In Fallon's analysis, Milton's writings reveal incremental stages between an adherence to orthodox dualism in the early poems and the final, heterodox concept of monism staked out in *De Doctrina Christiana* and realized in *Paradise Lost*, *Paradise Regained*, and *Samson Agonistes*. The great progression towards monism in Milton's thinking, Fallon argues, occurs in the divorce tracts of the 1640s.[5]

It will be one of my key assertions in the following pages that traces of Milton's monist materialism were already in evidence as early as 1629, the date of the Nativity Ode. Fallon's dismissal of the early poetry as unequivocally dualist is, in my estimation, too categorical an assessment.[6] I want to suggest instead that the early poems bear significant if unexpected traces of monist thinking, and that reassessing them in this light can contribute to a more nuanced, non-linear sense of Milton's complicated intellectual development.[7]

As important as that project, however, is the surprising nature of the traces themselves. No critical attention has, to my knowledge, been shown to the possibility that Milton's monism also animates his thinking about music.[8] Music is a constant, central, and highly developed theme in Milton's poetry, from the early Nativity Ode and "At a Solemn Music" to *Paradise Lost* and *Paradise Regained*. If Milton's representation of music in *Paradise Lost* is inflected by his monist materialism, then the depiction of music in the early poems will provide a comparative index of Milton's monist thinking. If, that is, Milton's representation of music in his later poetry can be classified as "monist," and his earlier representations of music correspond to his later representations, then we have solid evidence for monist tendencies earlier in Milton's career than previously realized. To assess that possibility, I will first analyze music as it is represented in *Paradise Lost*, and then turn back to Milton's earlier poetry. My analysis will evaluate two dimensions of music as Milton represents it: ontology, or the nature of its being; and agency, the nature of the action it achieves.

At stake is both a reading of Milton's intellectual development and also a sense of what distinguishes Milton's materialist model of music from that of his early modern contemporaries. Whereas for Thomas Wright and other relatively conservative thinkers, the material dimension of music must be jealously guarded against contaminating contact with the human soul, Milton embraces the materiality of music to the degree that it helps him conceive a fully materialist monist cosmos in which even the human soul is corporeal. Far from being suspicious of music as a materialist phenomenon, Milton makes music the decisive link in the material chain of being that extends from the merest stone all the way to God's body. Finally, music is not just made of matter; it is the particular matter that fuels the development of Milton's monist materialist universe.

What might "monist music," music operating under the rules of animist materialism, sound like? In tracing the development of Milton's monism, Stephen Fallon briefly attends to the discussion of music in Milton's 1644 prose tract, "Of Education." In what seems a clear echo of Platonic theory, Milton suggests that hearing or playing music after exercise or meals has a beneficial effect on students.[9] Fallon argues that Milton is here approaching, but not yet fully espousing, a materialist conception of the soul. Citing physically suggestive phrases in Milton's account of music, such as "*composing their travail'd spirits*" and "send their *mindes* backe to study *in good tune*" (qtd. in Fallon 88; emphasis Fallon's), Fallon deduces that Milton has at least begun to think of the soul as a physical entity:

> While editors normally point to Plato and Aristotle [as the basis for Milton's portrayal of music's effects], a more pertinent parallel

is Francis Bacon, who [...] attributed those effects to music's power to move (literally) the corporeal spirits [...]. Like Bacon, Milton follows Plato and Aristotle on the effects of music but suggests that the medium of the effect is corporeal motion.

(Fallon 88–9)

Fallon's persuasive mode of analysis can be productively extended to *Paradise Lost*, where, as we shall see, music *moves* the souls of the angels and of Adam and Eve.

In Book IV, when Eve asks Adam about why the stars shine during the night, Adam evokes the nocturnal music of angels:

> Millions of spiritual creatures walk the earth
> Unseen, both when we wake, and when we sleep:
> All these with ceaseless praise his works behold
> Both day and night: how often from the steep
> Of echoing hill or thicket have we heard
> Celestial voices to the midnight air,
> Sole, or responsive each to other's note
> Singing their great creator: oft in bands
> While they keep watch, or nightly rounding walk
> With heavenly touch of instrumental sounds
> In full harmonic number joined, their songs
> Divide the night, and lift our thoughts to heaven.
> (*PL* 4.677–88)[10]

Adam proclaims that the angelic music of praise continually "lift[s] our thoughts to heaven," "both when we wake, and when we sleep." This description seems a textbook case of Platonic musical theory, as heavenly music of praise induces a kind of psychosomatic effect on human rational processes. But a more complex reading emerges when it is recalled that for Milton, "thoughts" is a near synonym for "soul": as Raphael later tells Adam, "the soul / Reason receives, and *reason is her being*" (5.486–7, emphasis added). If Milton's monism holds that the body consists in the soul, it also stipulates that the soul consists in rational thought. In operating on *thoughts*, then, music is operating on the substance of the soul, and its effect is physical: songs "*lift* our thoughts to heaven" (emphasis added). What first strikes the reader as a figurative Platonic account of music emerges on closer scrutiny as a monist image, the erection of the corporeal soul into a form "nearer tending" to God (5.476). The agency of music already accomplishes in part what Raphael suggests God may someday fully realize: the conversion of human substance into the more refined ethereal substance of angels.[11, 12]

Within the monist universe of *Paradise Lost*, then, Milton utilizes the agency of music with respect to the soul to emphasize the material ontology of the soul. In Adam's account, Milton also extends his animist materialism to encompass sound itself, in a manner that both resonates with the thought of contemporaries like Thomas Wright who saw music as a material phenomenon, and carries it further through Milton's characteristic blend of rigor and intellectual adventurousness. Adam's description of sound makes use of conceptual terms that suggest it functions as a physical, material object. Adam notes with an aficionado's ear that the angels sing in a complex choral configuration, "sole, or responsive each to other's note." The sonic picture implies a formal complexity in which melody can either stand alone as monophony or seamlessly intertwine with other monophonic strands to create a rich polyphony that Adam calls "full harmonic number." This complex pattern of recombination makes use of the conceptual framework of geometry, implying musical parts as independent shapes that can be integrated into a unified larger shape. But if music has the property of shape, or *form*, it also has the property of *accident*—external texture that gives form material presence. Adam describes the rich timbral variegation of angelic music, as "instrumental sounds" are often added to the a cappella "celestial voices." By giving it the philosophical properties of form and accident, Milton suggests that music behaves as a physical object. Milton's choice of a physical verb for the interaction of music with its environment emphasizes this sense of musical sound as a material object: "their songs / *Divide* the night" (4.687–8, emphasis added).

In both agency and in ontology, music as Adam describes it comports with Milton's animist materialism. The agency of music on the soul confirms the soul's material nature, while music itself then takes on a material ontology, to the point where sound itself can act as physical matter in dividing the night. In Milton's materialist universe, the material effect of music on the soul reveals music itself as made of matter. Here is where Milton stands apart from Wright and other conservative thinkers; rather than shying away from the specter of a material soul raised by a materialist concept of music, Milton uses music to reveal the materiality of the soul, which in turn confirms that music operates as matter.

Adam's account of music is not an isolated phenomenon in *Paradise Lost*. Wherever music is heard, it operates as a material object and has a discernible effect on the substance of its listeners' souls. This effect can be either good or bad. In Hell, the infernal music of the fallen angels hardens them further against God:

> Others more mild,
> Retreated in a silent valley, sing
> With notes angelical to many a harp
> Their own heroic deeds and hapless fall
> By doom of battle; and complain that fate
> Free virtue should enthral to force or chance.
> Their song was partial, but the harmony
> (What could it less when spirits immortal sing?)
> Suspended hell, and took with ravishment
> The thronging audience.
>
> (*PL* 2.546–555)

The music of complaint is described in conceptual terms consistent with Adam's. Like angelic music, this infernal music is imagined as a physical object with both accident—e.g., the timbral variegation of harps—and form: the progressive harmony that "suspended hell."[13] But while its accident is similar to that of unfallen music—the demons produce "notes angelical"—in its specific form infernal music differs from the heavenly song. Unlike angelic music, infernal music is not properly choral; instead, it is "partial," produced in disjunct parts that, while they do combine in "harmony," remain musically exclusive from one another—as the "sole" yet "responsive" singers of the heavenly chorus did not.[14] With its "notes angelical," the music of the demons has the accident of heavenly music and might seduce the unwary listener into believing it to be such; but its underlying form, not immediately apparent to the ear, makes clear that infernal music is ontologically dangerously different from the music of the unfallen angels.

Infernal music does not "lift" the thoughts of the fallen angels to heaven. Instead, it "took with ravishment / The thronging audience" (2.554–5). This action offers a precise contrast with Adam's observation of the effects of angelic music. *Ravishment* here means "ecstasy, delight; […] the fact of being entranced or captivated" (*OED* 2.a). In Milton's monist universe, ravishment *imprisons* the soul with sensual delight. Good angelic music raises the soul into free rationality, lifting *thoughts* to heaven and thus refining man's substance to a more ethereal, angel-like consistency; fallen angelic music abases the soul into nonrational pleasure and by implication hardens the corporeal substance of the fallen angels into an imprisoning container. Even as these fallen angels complain that fate has subjected their power of free will to God's tyranny or to pure chance ("[Others] complain that fate / Free virtue should *enthral* to force or chance" [2.550–1, emphasis added]), they *choose* to abandon themselves to an imprisoning hedonism. The angels freely chose to fall just as they now freely choose to produce music that enthralls their "free virtue."

The parallel accounts of heavenly and infernal music suggest that in *Paradise Lost* the basic phenomenon of sound behaves like the primordial matter on which the original act of Creation was performed. When God retired himself from infinitude, what was left behind was chaotic matter, bereft of his goodness and subject to "necessity and chance" (7.172; see 7.165–173). When God sends the Son out to shape the matter of chaos into the universe and its contents, chaotic matter becomes once again *good*. But morally neutral matter can become either good or bad. Man was originally good until his fall, after which, for Milton, his very matter became corrupt; original sin is a material corruption transmitted from parents to child (*The Christian Doctrine*, *CPW* VI 318–22).[15] The contrasting musics of the good angels and the fallen angels suggest that making music is an act of creation that shapes the morally neutral matter of sound into either good or bad form.

If music-making is a creative act that echoes the supreme act of divine creation, then music itself, once created, retains in its material nature a further creative potency to influence other matter by adjusting it towards good or evil. This creative power to affect other matter operates not only on living beings such as Adam and Eve, but even on the geographic substance of the natural world around them, as Adam and Eve themselves realize in their morning orison:

> Witness if I be silent, morn or even,
> To hill, or valley, fountain, or fresh shade
> Made vocal by my song, and taught his praise.
> (*PL* 5.202–4)

Adam and Eve's creative production of sound as good music influences the matter of the landscape in which they stand. This response is no mere echo. Instead, in Adam and Eve's account, the "hill, or valley, fountain, or fresh shade" approach the animacy of living beings. Adam and Eve hear that their song causes the matter of the landscape to become "vocal," that is, to take on the capacity to utter coherent sounds, and, further, that in so doing the putatively inanimate landscape completes what is properly a rational activity: being "taught" how to praise God.[16] To be clear, I am not suggesting that Adam and Eve's song takes on the creative power of God Himself in making the natural world animate. But I think, if we recall Fallon's concept of animist materialism, that Milton is indeed suggesting a more profound effect than an echo. What is implied is that Adam and Eve's song of praise slightly refines the material substance of the landscape so that it tends nearer to God.

Milton provides a formal mimesis for this refining power of good music. In Adam and Eve's 56-line morning orison (5.153–208), the word *praise* occurs as a line-ending no fewer than six times (ll. 172, 184, 191, 196, 199, 204). The rime-riche effect is further amplified by a variety of line-ending words that produce close slant-rhymes with the word *praise*—e.g., "flies" (176), "rise" (185, 188), and "shade" (203)—some of which present their own rime-riche pairings. For a poet who famously rejects the "jingling sound of like endings" as "the troublesome and modern bondage of rhyming" (Milton, "The Verse" p. 55),[17] this passage represents a calculated departure from blank verse. Even as Adam and Eve claim their song has the power to transform the matter of the natural world around them, Milton ratifies their claim by allowing that song to transform the normative blank-verse terrain of his poem. Like the diegetic landscape, the material substance of the poem is itself refined so that its line-endings begin to rhyme. Like the diegetic landscape, the poetic landscape is quite literally "taught his *praise*" (emphasis added). The mimetic effect achieved by rhyme, as the word *praise* or its slant-rhyme equivalents proliferate throughout the passage, demonstrates for the reader the creative power of music to give new shape to other matter.

That power, a hallmark of music in the monist universe of *Paradise Lost*, is precisely what the younger poet emphasizes almost forty years earlier in his account of divine music in the "Ode on the Morning of Christ's Nativity" (1629):

> Ring out ye crystal spheres,
> Once bless our human ears,
>   (If ye have power to touch our senses so)
> And let your silver chime
> Move in melodious time;
>   And let the base of heaven's deep organ blow,
> And with your ninefold harmony
> Make up full consort to the angelic symphony.
>
> For if such holy song
> Enwrap our fancy long,
>   Time will run back, and fetch the age of gold,

>   And speckled vanity
>   Will sicken soon and die,
>   And lep'rous sin will melt from earthly mould,
>   And hell itself will pass away,
>   And leave her dolorous mansions to the peering day.
>   ("On the Morning of Christ's
>   Nativity" ll. 125–40)[18]

The speaker imagines the power of celestial music to effect a material change in the substance of the fallen world: "speckled vanity" will sicken and die even as the "earthly mould" will be purged of the corruptions of sin; the entire geography of Hell will be dissolved into sunlight. This material potency anticipates the creative agency of music as Milton later imagines it in his materialist epic universe. It does not, however, fully conform to that model. The speaker in the Nativity Ode suggests that he is only imagining the material agency of celestial music, and that this imaginative vision (rather than any real physical consequences) is actually what the music brings about: "For if such holy song / Enwrap our fancy long, / Time will run back" (emphasis added). At this early stage in his intellectual development, Milton remains tentative enough about the material agency of music that he relegates it to a poetic flight of "fancy."

Similarly, Milton's mature musical ontology is here present in qualified terms. At first glance, it seems that Milton conceptualizes music as physical, having both form and accident. In formal terms, the "ninefold harmony" of the crystal spheres is complemented by the further harmonic strand of "heaven's deep organ"; the result is the "full consort" of the "angelic symphony." As for accident, Milton uses the synesthetic epithet, "*silver* chime" (emphasis added), which appeals to the sense of sight to convey the accidental texture of music. But somehow music in the Nativity Ode does not quite take on the physical, material immediacy that is its distinctive feature in *Paradise Lost*. The reason, I think, is that unlike the extraordinary, freshly imagined musical imagery of *Paradise Lost*, the younger Milton resorts to stock images drawn from Classical cosmology and poetic cliché. In *Paradise Lost*, Milton asks the reader to imagine the exciting formal possibility of a chorus at once "sole" and "responsive each to other's note" (*PL* 4.683). Here, however, the poet resorts to borrowing the well-known Ptolemaic, originally Pythagorean, concept of the music of the nine spheres.[19] Not only is the image generic; "ninefold harmony" is an evocative epithet rather than an attempt to describe a real harmonic form. Similarly, "silver" is a clichéd rather than original descriptor for the sound of music, and is again evocative rather than specifying a precise musical sound. Without the mature Milton's bolder inventiveness, this music does not, in its form and accident, quite take on the physical presence of material music in *Paradise Lost*. And as with its material agency, the acoustic picture of celestial music is qualified as an imaginative vision within the poem, a mere product of fancy.

In that very act of qualification, however, Milton anticipates a key aspect of his later monism. As Fallon notes, Milton's conception of the body/soul formation is explicitly dualist in the Nativity Ode: The speaker refers to the body as "a darksome house of mortal clay" (l. 14), a house in which the disjunct soul lives (Fallon, *Milton among the Philosophers* 80). But in his account of a vision induced by music, the young poet introduces a physiological mechanism that implies the connection of body and soul. The speaker first describes the sensory apprehension of music—"Once bless our human *ears*, / (If ye have power to *touch* our *senses* so)" (emphasis added)—and then wonders what might happen if "such holy song / *Enwrap* our *fancy* long" (emphasis added). The auditory sensory stimulus on the body's senses is a *touch* that seamlessly *enwraps* our *fancy*—that is, the imaginative faculty of the soul.[20] The tactile verbs, *touch* and *enwrap*, at least glance at some material connection between body and soul, however figurative the usage. Milton is almost certainly not here consciously monist, but I would argue that as he thinks about music and depicts it in his early poetry, he begins to anticipate the nature of a fully monist materialist universe.

That anticipation is even more pronounced in another early lyric, "At a Solemn Music" (1633?).[21] The agency of divine music on the soul is imagined in terms strikingly similar to Adam's account, published over thirty years later:

> Blest pair of sirens, pledges of heaven's joy,
> Sphere-borne harmonious sisters, Voice, and Verse,
> Wed your divine sounds, and mixed power employ
> Dead things with inbreathed sense able to pierce,
> And to our high-raised phantasy present,
> That undisturbed song of pure concent.
> ("At a Solemn Music" ll. 1–6)

Milton's speaker adjures the allegorical figures of heavenly music, Voice (sound) and Verse (text), to present their intertwined "divine sounds" to human beings on earth. Hearing this "undisturbed song of pure concent" has a remarkable effect on human beings: it raises high their *phantasy* (i.e., *fantasy*), a word synonymous with *fancy* in the Nativity

Ode.[22] If Fallon were to analyze this passage, he would surely note that Milton describes the operation of music on the soul in terms at least as suggestively physical as those in "Of Education"—but a full decade earlier. In fact, the language of the lyric more precisely corresponds to Milton's later monist vision. Just as Adam in *Paradise Lost* notes that angelic songs "*lift* our thoughts to heaven" (4.688, emphasis added), the speaker of "At a Solemn Music" claims that heavenly song *raises*, or erects, the mental faculties.

Also as in *Paradise Lost*, music in "At a Solemn Music" possesses the material agency to animate entities that are not alive. In *Paradise Lost* that power is formulated as making the inanimate landscape "vocal"; in the early lyric, the formulation is an allusion to the Orpheus myth, in which the bard could bring rocks and other inanimate natural objects to life: "Wed your divine sounds, and mixed power employ / Dead things with inbreathed sense able to pierce" (3–4). The power to pierce the matter of "dead things" with *inbreathed sense* is more than an allusion to Orpheus; it is a statement of the creative agency of music that anticipates the terms Milton will use in the *Christian Doctrine* for the divine act of Creation itself: God's *breathing* of life into the matter of his creatures.[23] The imaginative work of rendering music in poetry encourages the young Milton to think about both music and the soul in ways that correspond to a philosophical system he would not formally enunciate for several decades.

If the agency of music in "At a Solemn Music" looks ahead to *Paradise Lost*, in representing the ontology of music, Milton again closely anticipates his mature thinking. Just as in *Paradise Lost*, music is evoked in conceptual terms that suggest a physical object with both form and accident. The form of the "melodious noise" of heavenly music is constructed by wedding the divine sounds of Voice (musical setting) and Verse (text); the accidental texture is described at length in richly material terms ("the bright seraphim in burning row / Their loud uplifted angel trumpets blow, / And the cherubic host in thousand choirs / Touch their immortal harps of golden wires" [10–13][24]). And just as neutral sound in *Paradise Lost* is shaped into the form of either good or bad music, so, too, is sound in "At a Solemn Music" wrought into either moral or immoral music: "Wed your divine sounds, and mixt power employ," Milton's speaker pleads with the harmonious Sisters, Voice and Verse:

> That we on earth with undiscording voice
> May rightly answer that melodious noise;
> As once we did, till disproportioned sin

> Jarred against nature's chime, and with harsh din
> Broke the fair music that all creatures made
> To their great Lord, whose love their motion swayed
> In perfect diapason, whilst they stood
> In first obedience, and their state of good.
> ("At a Solemn Music", ll. 3; 17–24)

The "melodious noise" of heavenly music is contrasted with the "harsh din" produced by "disproportioned sin." Marrying a good text to a proper musical setting shapes sound into "melodious noise"; but the action of sin, by contrast, is "disproportioned," or inharmonious, and its dissonant clash with "nature's chime" results in a "harsh din." This bad music, in turn, has the further material effect of shattering the "fair music" made by prelapsarian creatures.

This dichotomy of the ontology and agency of good and bad music would seem to match Milton's later conception in *Paradise Lost*, but there is, once again, an important qualification. In "At a Solemn Music," while the "melodious noise" of heavenly music is described as a literal acoustic phenomenon, the "harsh din" made by sin is not. By literal acoustic phenomenon, I refer not to whether music is being given form and accident as a physical object, but rather to whether music is heard within the poetic reality or used as a figure of rhetoric. When "disproportioned sin" breaks the "fair music" once made by obedient creatures, the reader is not being directed to imagine that the fall of man was a musical event in which dissonance interrupted the prelapsarian symphony. Instead, the reader quickly grasps that Milton is speaking in a metaphoric register, in which dissonant music serves as a metaphor for disobedience to God. As Milton gives voice to a moral vision opposing heavenly obedience to God with fallen, sinful disobedience, music modulates in his poem from being represented as a real acoustic object to being represented as a metaphor.[25]

In the 1634 *Masque* he wrote to be performed at Ludlow Castle, however, Milton retains his conception of music as ethically charged—produced by and expressive of good or evil—while consistently and vividly evoking sound as a real, not metaphoric, acoustic phenomenon. The friendly guardian spirit, disguised as the shepherd Thyrsis, gives the Brothers an account of two contrasting musical performances. First, the spirit describes the "light fantastic round" of Comus (l. 144):

> The wonted roar was up amidst the woods,
> And filled the air with barbarous dissonance
> At which I ceased, and listened them a while,

> Till an unusual stop of sudden silence
> Gave respite to the drowsy frighted steeds.

Then he describes the music sung by the Lady who is sister to the two young men:

> At last a soft and solemn-breathing sound
> Rose like a steam of rich distilled perfumes,
> And stole upon the air, that even Silence
> Was took ere she was ware, and wished she might
> Deny her nature, and be never more
> Still to be so displaced. I was all ear,
> And took in strains that might create a soul
> Under the ribs of death.
>   (*A Masque presented at Ludlow Castle,*
>   *1634* ll. 548–52; 554–561)

The spirit's account of the contrasting musics of Comus and the Lady recapitulates the musical properties delineated in the earlier lyric poems while rendering music as a fully material acoustic phenomenon. Comus and his band of followers shape sound into the form of "barbarous dissonance" with the accident of a "wonted roar." But this immoral music is also a real acoustic object that literalizes the figurative "harsh din" of "At a Solemn Music" as a "barbarous dissonance" which (note the physical verb) "*filled* the air" (emphasis added). This dissonance, in turn, is demonstrated to have powerful agency on the "frighted steeds."

The rich description of the Lady's song is even more evocative in laying out the material ontology of music and its resulting agency. Milton does not need to rely on the conceptual framework of form and accident to imply a physical body, but instead directly describes the sound of music in physical, even animate, terms. The Lady's act of singing is an act of "breathing sound" so that it is "soft and solemn." The Lady's transcendent creative art makes the acoustic phenomenon of music seem almost to take on life itself, to breathe. Once that "breathing sound" emerges into its environment, Milton describes it as a physical object, rising through the air "like a steam of rich distilled perfumes." Unlike the hackneyed synesthetic modifier "silver" in the Nativity Ode, the synesthetic description of sound dispersing like aroma is to my knowledge unique in this period, and, what is more, viscerally evocative of music as highly refined, ethereal matter.

As the Spirit's account continues, Milton adopts an allegorical mode of description that might seem to retreat from materialism. The Lady's "soft and solemn-breathing sound" surprises the personified allegorical figure of Silence, and is presumably so pleasing to this allegorical entity that she longs to deny her own nature as a lack of sound. Yet the allegorical mode is in fact, counterintuitively, a rhetorical move employed by the Spirit more vividly to evoke the material effect of the Lady's song as it disperses through its physical environment. By personifying the abstract concept of Silence, Milton translates an absence into a physical presence that can then interact with the materiality of the Lady's music: Silence "wished she might [...] be never more / Still *to be so displaced*" (emphasis added). With Silence as a displaceable physical entity, Milton can emphasize the physical presence of sound.[26]

The poet continues to avail himself of the allegorical mode as the Spirit says he "took in strains that might create a soul / Under the ribs of death" (560–1). This claim confronts us with what seems like incontrovertible evidence of a dualist philosophy: The soul is imagined as an entity distinct from the personified body of Death. But with the Spirit's claim that the Lady's good music potentially has the material agency to endow Death with a soul, Milton is thinking in monist terms in at least two respects. The first is the power of music to animate inanimate entities. Death is the ultimate absence of life; to create a soul in Death is the ultimate affirmation of the power of music: to pierce dead things, as Milton expresses it in "At a Solemn Music," with "inbreathed sense" ("At a Solemn Music" 4). The second element of monist thinking is a more profound anticipation of Milton's representational strategy in *Paradise Lost*. Death appears as a character in Milton's epic, and he stands with his mother Sin as the only fully realized allegorical entities in the poem. While allegorical characters, who are composed of abstract concepts rather than matter, would seem to deny the animist materialism underpinning Milton's universe, Stephen Fallon argues that Milton's use of Death and Sin actually confirms the poet's overarching materialist ontology. Because pure evil itself is, according to Augustine, the "privation of entity," Milton represents Death and Sin as allegories so as to register their lack of material substance (Fallon 168, 171).[27] Allegories have no matter, and hence have no soul. In these terms, Milton anticipates his materialist concept of soulless allegory in the 1634 *Masque*. Without the Lady's song, no soul exists in Death. Once again, the imaginative task of trying to represent music and its effects induces Milton to think in terms that he would later formalize as a rigorous philosophical system. These early poetic traces of Milton's intellectual development suggest that thinking about music, as much as thinking about divorce or the nature of Creation, fueled the evolution of Milton's philosophy from dualist to monist.

I have thus far been exploring how Milton's poetic depictions of music explicitly drive his patterns of thought towards monism and the larger system of animist materialism. There is, however, a feature of Milton's treatment of music that forms not an explicit but an implicit relation with his monism. Recall that in "At a Solemn Music" Milton initially evokes music as a real acoustic object but then shifts into metaphoric representation as the literal "melodious noise" becomes the figurative "harsh din" of the Fall (18, 20). The shift into metaphor, however, is not permanent in the poem. At the close of the lyric, Milton merges the acoustic and metaphoric dimensions of music in a vision of man's redemption:

> O may we soon again renew that song,
> And keep in tune with heaven, till God ere long
> To his celestial consort us unite,
> To live with him, and sing in endless morn of light.
>   ("At a Solemn Music" ll. 25–28)

In the final vision of the poem, as the speaker hopes that fallen humanity will renew our prelapsarian song, music is both metaphorical and a real acoustic event. If we redeemed humans can learn, metaphorically, to "keep in tune with heaven," the saved will quite literally join the celestial consort to participate in the real divine music-making richly described earlier in the poem. The "celestial consort" is in tune with God, literally and figuratively. Milton thus presents a model of music in which sound is simultaneously an acoustic phenomenon and a metaphor for a creature's relationship with God. This strikingly original model of simultaneous identity, achieved at the close of "At a Solemn Music," consistently governs Milton's subsequent depictions of music throughout his career, from *A Masque* (1634) until *Paradise Regained* (1671). In the next chapter, I will trace in detail the development of that model and its significance in Milton's thought.

For now, we can note that in its distinctive elision of the traditional division between the sensory phenomenon of sound and the intellectual phenomenon of meaning, this model presents an analogy with the mature Milton's monist model, which elided the traditional division between body and soul. "The whole man is the soul, and the soul the man," declares Milton in *The Christian Doctrine* (*CPW* VI 318). Music is at once soul—a metaphoric valence—and body, a sonorous acoustic presence. The two components are not, ultimately, separable. This relation is, of course, only analogous; I am not suggesting, although there are intriguing traces of such a suggestion in the account of the Lady's song, that Milton considered music a living being with a body and a soul. But I am suggesting that thinking about music as existing simultaneously in two dimensions that are somehow both distinct and overlapping provided Milton with an intellectual structure conducive to reasoning about the resistant concept of a human ontology inhering in two dimensions that are somehow both separate and unified. As Fallon sympathetically says of *The Christian Doctrine*, "Milton struggles…to articulate monism with a vocabulary tempered by centuries of dualism" (Fallon 102). Fallon means, I think, not only the problem of describing the nature of monism but also the mental difficulty of *thinking* about monism within an inherited philosophical discourse that systematically schematized body and soul as separate concepts. For Milton, music provided a surrogate discourse in which he could reason exploratively about the unity of seemingly separate things without the conceptual baggage of inherited Christian theology. Whether Milton ever recognized the analogy between his model of music and his model of human and divine ontology is not, ultimately, important. Probably he did not. What is important, however, is that in addition to the explicit ways explored above in which representing music in poetry influenced Milton's development of monism and animist materialism, it is also apparent that thinking about music afforded the poet with an opportunity, perhaps available nowhere else in his intellectual life, to come to rational terms with one of the central paradoxes of his mature theology.

Notes

1 See Gordon Teskey, *Delirious Milton*, Chapter 5: "God's Body: Concept and Metaphor" (Cambridge: Harvard UP, 2006), 86–106.
2 See Gina Bloom, *Voice in Motion* (Philadelphia: U Pennsylvania P, 2007). Bloom examines both Shakespeare and Marston as well as sermons and scientific pamphlets. Like other recent scholars of early modern sound, Bloom focuses on the gendered dimension of embodied sound, and in particular the female voice; for a representative collection, see *Gender and Song in Early Modern England*, edited by Leslie C. Dunn and Katherine R. Larson (Farnham/Burlington: Ashgate, 2014).
3 For an overview of how the idea of "cosmic harmony" developed from its classical sources through to early modern Europe, see Jacomien Prins and Maude Vanhaelen, eds., *Sing Aloud Harmonious Spheres: Renaissance Conceptions of Cosmic Harmony* (New York/London: Routledge, 2018).

4 I quote from the revised 1604 edition of *The Passions of the Mind* (London, 1604), lightly modernizing orthography and silently emending printing errors. I am grateful to an anonymous manuscript reviewer for the press for pointing me to Wright's text as a central source for early modern debates about music, matter, and the soul, and for suggesting that Milton's monist account of music, as I describe it, solves the problem Wright articulates in these passages.

5 See *Milton among the Philosophers*, chapter 3: "Material Life: Milton's Animist Materialism" (Ithaca, NY: Cornell UP, 1991), 79–110; for extended treatment of the development of monism in the divorce tracts, see Fallon's "The Metaphysics of Milton's Divorce Tracts," in *Politics, Poetics, and Hermeneutics in Milton's Prose* (ed. David A. Loewenstein and James Grantham Turner; Cambridge: Cambridge UP, 1990), 69–83. For discussion of the contemporary philosophical debate involving the Hobbesian mechanist universe and its threat to the concept of free will, see *Milton among the Philosophers*, chapters 1–3 and 8. In *The Life of John Milton*, Barbara Lewalski integrates Fallon's argument about monism into a broader assessment of Milton's intellectual development, including the evolution of his views on Trinitarianism, Arianism, and Arminianism (see, e.g., Lewalski 414–415; Oxford: Blackwell, 2003).

6 Although Fallon does note that in the relatively early Ludlow *Masque* (1634) "the seeds of change are already present," he classifies earlier poems both Latin and English—including "In Obitum Praesulis Eliensis" (1626), the Nativity Ode (1629), *Il Penseroso* (1631?), and *Arcades* (1632)—as unambiguously dualist (Fallon, *Milton among the Philosophers* 81, 80).

7 In the other foundational book on Milton's materialism, *The Matter of Revolution: Science, Poetry, and Politics in the Age of Milton*, John Rogers accepts Fallon's account of Milton's development as a monist: "from 1650 to 1652 [...] Milton had not yet begun a formal articulation of his monistic materialism [...] an early engagement of the monistic union of body and spirit can be detected in Milton's divorce pamphlets (1643–45) and the *Areopagitica* (1644)" (Rogers 103, 104; Ithaca, NY: Cornell UP, 1996). More recently, in *"Matter of Glorious Trial": Spiritual and Material Substance in Paradise Lost* (New Haven: Yale, 2009), N. K. Sugimura has differed from Fallon and Rogers by arguing for a nonlinear and less clear-cut assessment of Milton's ontological views: "it is an error to say that Milton believes in either monism or dualism. Milton's poetry does not present us with a question of either/or but of an and. While parts of Milton's poetry may confirm a monist materialist reading, other parts do not. The main methodological point of difference between my book and those that have preceded it is that I reject the idea that one can create a continuous intellectual genealogy for Milton's poetry" (Sugimura xvi). In her reconsideration of the relation between poetry and philosophy in Milton, Sugimura does consider works predating the divorce tracts, such as the Ludlow *Masque*, but her concerns are to investigate Milton's Platonism versus his Aristotelianism. The impact of Sugimura's work is still being considered; for now, I adhere to Fallon as

the standard account. Prior to Sugimura, Rogers, and Fallon, the topic of Milton's monism was explored by Rumrich (*Matter of Glory: A New Preface to Paradise Lost*, Pittsburgh: U Pittsburgh P, 1987).

8 I am indebted to the late Barbara Lewalski for this suggestion, which was the basis for this chapter. In conversation, Professor Lewalski further suggested that the early poetry might bear traces of monist thinking even though Milton had not yet arrived at or fully articulated that concept. In 2010, Beverley Sherry did consider the relation between Milton's mature monist materialism and what she calls the "sound of *Paradise Lost*," but while she attends briefly to the music represented in the poem, her primary concern is to listen to the poem itself as material sound. See Sherry, "Milton, Materialism, and the Sound of *Paradise Lost*," *Essays in Criticism* 60.3 (July 2010), 220–241. Katherine Cox's 2016 essay, "'How cam'st thou speakable of mute': Satanic Acoustics in *Paradise Lost*," considers a complementary way of thinking about the materiality of sound in *Paradise Lost*: the acoustic production of sound via meteorological pressure through instruments—a phenomenon that Cox shows is related to demonic being in *Paradise Lost*. Cox's work combines acoustical science and the study of musical instruments, subjects outside my frame of reference in this book. Cox does not consider, as I do, music with respect to the philosophical ontology of monist or animist materialism. See Cox, "'How cam'st thou speakable of mute': Satanic Acoustics in *Paradise Lost*," *Milton Studies* 57 (2016), 233–260.

9 See introduction to this book.

10 All references to *Paradise Lost* are to the Longman second edition, edited by Alastair Fowler.

11 Raphael says to Adam: "And from these corporal nutriments perhaps / Your bodies may at last turn all to spirit, / Improved by tract of time, and winged ascend / Ethereal, as we" (5.496–9).

12 David Ainsworth makes a similar claim that music in *Paradise Lost* has a material effect on the conjoined body and soul, but Ainsworth's emphasis is on a kind of simulated *transport* rather than a material refinement: "Milton's monist rapture in *Paradise Lost* transports or transforms the physical substance that constitutes both body and soul together, either lifting the subject as a whole to heaven, or causing a change in that subject's state, which temporarily renders his or her present location as heaven in much the same way that Satan always inhabits hell regardless of his physical surroundings" (Ainsworth, "Rapturous Milton" 149). Where I understand the effect of music as refining human material being in the manner Raphael describes, Ainsworth contends that music causes the human being "as a whole" to be lifted to heaven, an imaginative claim I do not quite understand. See Ainsworth, "Rapturous Milton and the Communal Harmony of Faith," *Milton Quarterly* 47.3, 149–62.

13 *Suspension* refers to a particular technique of musical harmony whereby a pitch, consonant in one chord, is carried over, or *suspended*, so that it becomes dissonant in a new chord. The *suspension* is then resolved in the

new chord by stepwise motion from the dissonant pitch to a triadic, consonant pitch. The *OED* notes the first usage of "suspension" as a technical harmonic term only in the eighteenth century, however, so Milton may not have known the term in its modern technical musical sense ("suspension, *n*.I.8.").

14 It is not quite clear precisely what musical form Milton may be describing here. Drawing on the key word "partial," Stephen Buhler argues that the musical style of the fallen angels' music is polyphonic, while the songs of the loyal angels in heaven "most likely involve homophony" (Buhler, "Counterpoint" 20). I am not fully convinced by this potentially reductive division; does Milton wish to slot angelic and prelapsarian earthly music into early modern stylistic categories? Milton devotes considerable energy to striving to imagine prelapsarian aesthetic forms beyond fallen human comprehension, and I suspect that he is trying to do so with music. See chapter 2 for an extended comparison between infernal and heavenly music, including a fuller consideration of Buhler's argument.

15 For helping me to understand God's difficult speech in Book 7, I am grateful to Gordon Teskey. See Teskey, "God's Body: Concept and Metaphor," chapter 5 in *Delirious Milton* (Cambridge: Harvard UP, 2006), 86–106.

16 The *OED* cites this usage as an instance of a generalized definition of grand sound: "Full of (vocal) sound; sounding, resounding" ("vocal, *adj.* A.I.7."). But I would submit that Milton uses the word in a way that also suggests "having the capacity to speak, sing [...] producing or uttering sounds," or even "conveying impressions or ideas as if by speech; expressive, eloquent" ("A.I.4., 5.").

17 As with all references to *Paradise Lost*, this citation of Milton's prefatory note on the verse is to Fowler's Longman edition (2nd rev. ed.); see pp. 54–55.

18 All references to Milton's poetry other than *Paradise Lost* are to the Longman second edition, ed. John Carey.

19 As Carey observes in his note on this passage, "The idea that each sphere of the universe produced a note as it revolved [...] was Pythagorean in origin" ("On the Morning of Christ's Nativity" ll. 125–35n).

20 *Fancy* has many denotative possibilities, but all of them imply a function of the mind, which, as the spirit, is a category of the soul rather than of the body. Earlier in the Nativity Ode, the speaker declares that music "all their souls in blissful rapture took" (98). The enwrapping of fancy is logically equivalent to the taking of souls in rapture, which in turn implies the qualified logical equivalence of "fancy" and "souls"—the qualification is that *fancy* corresponds to a specific operation of the soul, its imaginative capacity.

21 Like the Nativity Ode, "At a Solemn Music" first appeared in the *1645 Poems*. It has not been conclusively dated, but Carey assigns it tentatively to 1633, noting that "Suggested dates range from early 1631 [...] to Sept.–Oct. 1637" (*Complete Shorter Poems* p. 167). The earliest date thought possible thus places this lyric after Milton's own dating of the Nativity Ode to 1629.

Music as Matter 37

22 The *Oxford English Dictionary* notes that *fantasy* had a particular meaning in the context of scholastic psychology, a meaning Milton almost certainly would have known: "mental apprehension of an object of perception; the faculty by which this is performed" ("fantasy | phantasy, *n*.1.a."). In this particular denotation, the *OED* entry indicates, *fantasy* is precisely equivalent to *fancy*. This meaning was current through at least 1669.

23 See *CPW* VI 318.

24 The libretto for Handel's oratorio *Samson*, written by Newburgh Hamilton, lifts these lines in slightly altered form for the Israelite Woman's closing aria: "Let the bright Seraphim in burning row, / Their loud-uplifted angel trumpets blow. / Let the Cherubic host, in tuneful choirs / Touch their immortal harps with golden wires" (Hamilton and Handel 3.3). For a fuller account of the significance of this use of "At a Solemn Music" in *Samson*, see chapter 3 of this book.

25 See chapter 2 for an extended treatment of Milton's understanding of music as both metaphor and acoustic phenomenon.

26 The most powerful use of allegory in *A Masque* occurs at its close, with the entrance of Sabrina. Whereas Silence is merely a figure of rhetoric in "Thyrsis's" speech, Sabrina is a character in the masque—technically, she is a representative of chastity, but also, as Barbara Lewalski suggested to me in conversation, she is the allegorical embodiment of moral art, and most particularly, of moral music. Sabrina enters the stage while singing, and her verse as she frees the Lady is in a catalectic tetrameter meant to express musicality in contrast with the speech of other characters. Sabrina's appearance brings the material agency of music in *A Masque* to its apotheosis. Despite her Brothers' intervention and the temporary defeat of Comus, the Lady is still imprisoned in his chair, "In stony fetters fixed" (818). Only Sabrina can release the Lady, which she does, saying "this marble venomed seat / Smeared with gums of glutinous heat / I touch with chaste palms moist and cold, / Now the spell hath lost his hold" (915–919). Sabrina's touch succeeds where military force fails. Since Sabrina herself is an embodiment of good music centered on an ethos of chastity, the liberating touch of her chaste palm emerges as a vivid means of dramatizing the material agency of *good music*.

27 See *Milton among the Philosophers*, chapter 6: "Sin and Death: The Substance of Allegory," pp. 168–193. Fallon's stimulating discussion of the interplay between ontology and allegory is an important account of a fascinating subject meriting further study.

2 "Pure Concent"
Music as Sound and Metaphor

In the previous chapter, I investigated how Milton's efforts to depict music both track and stimulate the development of his monism. In so doing, Milton embraces the materiality of music—and its aesthetic and theological ramifications—in a way from which other more conservative contemporary thinkers recoiled. In the present chapter, I wish to concentrate more particularly on how Milton represents music as an aesthetic medium. By attending to how Milton describes music as an art form, we can gain new insight not only into Milton as an interdisciplinary thinker, but also into some of Milton's core concerns as a Christian poet. The most striking broad conclusion is that Milton's poetic accounts of music as a whole ultimately suggest a greater trust in music than in poetry as an artistic medium worthy of God. I am also concerned to show that there is a greater unity of thought underpinning Milton's accounts of music throughout his poetic output than has been noticed in prior criticism.

Why should a poet consider music a more reliably worthy medium than his own? If Milton relied on the expressive power of the arts to achieve his political and moral goals, he also always distrusted their potential to seduce fallen human beings into sensual abandonment. In music, I shall argue, Milton found an aesthetic object uniquely capable of reconciling sensuous beauty with Christian duty.

In the early lyric "At a Solemn Music," at which we glanced in the previous chapter, Milton first constructs a complex poetic model for music. Opening with an invocation to the pair of heavenly sirens, Milton adjures the "harmonious sisters" to present on earth the divine music hymned to God in heaven:

> Blest pair of sirens, pledges of heaven's joy,
> Sphere-born harmonious sisters, Voice, and Verse,

DOI: 10.4324/9781003378389-4

> Wed your divine sounds, and mixed power employ
> Dead things with inbreathed sense able to pierce,
> And to our high-raised phantasy present,
> That undisturbed song of pure concent,
> Ay sung before the sapphire-coloured throne
> To him that sits thereon.
> ("At a Solemn Music" ll. 1–8)

For Milton, the most ethically and aesthetically worthy music is not purely instrumental music, but rather, *song*—music with words. Personifying the musical and textual elements of song as a pair of heavenly sisters, "Voice," or music, and "Verse," poetry, Milton asks the sisters to merge their aesthetic elements and then to present to men on earth the highest form of this unified art: the "undisturbed song of pure concent" sung to God in heaven (6). The word *concent* is suggestive.[1] From Latin *concentenus*, "a singing together," *concent* is a musical term that can mean either literal harmony, i.e., "harmony of sounds; accord or concord of several voices or parts" (*OED*, "concent, *n*.1."), or, in a typically figurative sense, "agreement, accord, harmony" (*OED*, "concent, *n*.2."). Both denotations are linked by the idea that there is a harmonious correspondence between two or more elements that form a unified system. In Milton's phrase, the literal musical denotation of the word, *harmony*, is more obviously relevant, as the angelic hosts sing an "undisturbed song of pure *harmony*" that is euphonious rather than dissonant. Yet the figurative meaning is the more profound, suggesting that the angels form a unified group acting with a single purpose. Milton implies a further, yet more significant pun: our standard modern sense of *consent* as "voluntary agreement" (*OED*, "consent, *n*.1.a."). This denotation has a separate, post-classical Latin etymology and is less obviously at play in this passage (*OED*, "concent, *n*.," "consent, *n*.," "consent, *v*.").[2] But consent, or obedience, is a core principle—perhaps the core principle—of Milton's mature theology. Already the same sense of Miltonic obedience that undergirds the theodicy of *Paradise Lost* illuminates the unity of the angelic host in "At a Solemn Music." Their act of singing expresses the unified choice of the unfallen angels to *consent* to governance by God. These angels produce a song that—from the musical meaning of *concent*—emerges in perfectly tuned harmony, but their choice to sing in such accord also demonstrates their *pure consent*, their absolute obedience, to God. This pun defines divine song as music that is dual in nature. It is at once an acoustic phenomenon, that is, a physical, sonic event, yet it is also a metaphor, a representation of a political relationship with God.[3] This dual nature of divine song, as an acoustic phenomenon and a metaphor, governs the unfolding thematic structure of "At a Solemn Music."[4]

First, as Milton describes the heavenly music that he wishes the sirens to export from heaven to earth, the divine song is understood as primarily *aural*:

> Ay sung before the sapphire-coloured throne
> To him that sits thereon
> With saintly shout, and solemn jubilee,
> Where the bright seraphim in burning row
> Their loud uplifted angel trumpets blow,
> And the cherubic host in thousand choirs
> Touch their immortal harps of golden wires,
> With those just spirits that wear victorious palms,
> Hymns devout and holy psalms
> Singing everlastingly.
> ("At a Solemn Music" ll. 7–16)

Music is rendered as a literal, physical acoustic event: angelic singing accompanied by sonorous musical instruments. The terms are plainly not metaphoric.[5] But this literal music is heard only in heaven. If it were also heard on Earth, Milton imagines, its effect would be to reform the behavior of sinful humanity, to inspire by its sound a receptive state of ecstasy, "high-raised phantasy" (5), in which fallen humans would be induced to "rightly answer that melodious noise" (18).

As Milton exhorts the Sirens to present the angelic music on Earth, music itself shifts in the poem's system of representation from an acoustic phenomenon to a metaphoric expression of the relationship between God and his creatures. Let us hear angelic music on Earth, Milton urges, so "That we on Earth with undiscording voice / May rightly answer that melodious noise":

> As once we did, till disproportioned sin
> Jarred against nature's chime, and with harsh din
> Broke the fair music that all creatures made
> To their great Lord, whose love their motion swayed
> In perfect diapason, whilst they stood
> In first obedience, and their state of good.
> ("At a Solemn Music" ll. 17–24)

The poet imagines that, if heavenly music were heard on Earth, humans and all of God's creatures would be induced to resume their unfallen "state of good," standing, "[a]s once we did," "in first obedience." While music in the poem's vision of heaven is genuinely acoustic, music on Earth is a metaphor that expresses the standing of God's creatures with respect to God and the natural order that God has established. On the fallen Earth where Milton now lives, the "fair music that all creatures made" in the prelapsarian "state of good"—that is, the just obedience all creatures once showed to God—has been compromised by man's "disproportioned," or unharmonious, sin. Earthly existence is now in continual discord, a metaphorical symphony of ongoing sin.[6]

The poem has unfolded structurally by transforming music from its initial poetic representation as an acoustic event into a new representation as a metaphor that expresses both the former obedience and the current disobedience of man. In the final quatrain of the poem, Milton anticipates the ultimate redemption of man by wedding the separate acoustic and metaphoric representational dimensions of music into a unified form:

> O may we soon again renew that song,
> And keep in tune with heaven, till God ere long
> To his celestial consort us unite,
> To live with him, and sing in endless morn of light.
> ("At a Solemn Music" ll. 25–28)

At first, music remains merely metaphoric: Milton's hope is that, if "we," all people on Earth, "soon again renew that song"—if we metaphorically "keep in tune with heaven" by showing absolute obedience to God—then God will hasten our redemption. In imagining that ultimate redemption, however, Milton represents music as a rich duality, at once acoustic and metaphoric. The pivoting from the exclusively metaphoric sense of music to a new, dual sense occurs precisely at the phrase "celestial *consort*" (emphasis added)—another pun. *Consort* means both "a company or set of musicians" (*OED*, "*n.2* II.4") and "A partner in wedded or parental relations" (*OED*, "*n.1* 1.3"). If we humans show absolute obedience to God, Milton hopes, God will quite literally transport us up into heaven to join the ranks of the angelic choir—ranks in which we will once again constitute God's *consort*, his eternal partner, even as we physically participate in the musical performance the *consort* of angels produces. The final line of the poem at once schematizes and holds these two senses together via its delicately balanced caesura: "To live with him, ‖ and sing in endless morn of light." The singing by the joint choir of angels and redeemed humanity—God's *consort*—is at once the literal acoustic phenomenon described at the outset of the poem, and a metaphoric representation of perpetual obedience to God. By merging the acoustic and metaphoric dimensions of music, Milton provides a semantic mimesis for the redemption of man.

In order to accomplish that climactic mimetic merging of the dual dimensions of music, Milton must first present those dimensions separately in the poem. But elsewhere in his mature poetry, most strikingly in the comprehensively imagined universe of *Paradise Lost*, Milton conceived of all music as properly always having both an acoustic and metaphoric dimension *simultaneously*. Other critics have noted the metaphoric dimension of Milton's representation of music, most recently David Ainsworth, who argues persuasively that "music, as a communal exercise of harmonious association, both inspires and metaphorically represents heavenly rapture. Song and harmony thus stand in for, and can produce, Christian community and communion with God" (Ainsworth, "Rapturous Milton" 149). My claim is somewhat different: I argue that Milton in his representation of music balances a metaphoric dimension with an equally developed sensuous acoustics. Where Ainsworth is concerned with how music constitutes a metaphor for "Christian community," I am concerned with how music retains a visceral acoustic sensuousness even as it promotes Christian obedience.[7]

Modern physics provides a useful analogy for understanding Milton's conception of music. According to the wave-particle theory of light, the observer can think of light either as a wave or as a particle, called a photon, depending on the context in which light is observed. But while it suits the observer's purposes to construe light as either wave or photon, in reality, light is always, at once, paradoxically both a wave and a photon. Likewise, for Milton, music can be thought of in one of two ways depending on the context in which it figures; but, while it may suit one's poetic purposes to construe music as either acoustic phenomenon or metaphor, it is always, paradoxically, both at once. Although this simultaneous duality is made more explicit in *Paradise Lost*, "At a Solemn Music" implies the duality both with its final vision of the music made by redeemed humans, and with the puns that anchor the poem: *concent* and *consort*. As we saw, both words, as puns, identify music simultaneously as an acoustic phenomenon and as a metaphor.[8]

"At a Solemn Music" reveals that, for Milton, music can fuse sensuous aesthetic beauty with the moral obligation of Christian duty. In *Paradise Lost*, to which I turn next, Milton explores this satisfying fusion by realizing the model of music from "At a Solemn Music" on a grand scale.

Music resounds in the prelapsarian earthly realm of *Paradise Lost*. In their morning orison, an a cappella song "More tunable than needed lute or harp / To add more sweetness" (5.151–2), Adam and Eve evoke an entire universe reverberating with music in praise of God:

> Thou sun, of this great world both eye and soul,
> Acknowledge him thy greater, sound his praise [...]
> ....
> His praise ye winds, that from four quarters blow,
> Breathe soft or loud; and wave your tops, ye pines,
> With every plant, in sign of worship wave.
> Fountains and ye, that warble, as ye flow,
> Melodious murmurs, warbling tune his praise.
> Join voices all ye living souls, ye birds,
> That singing up to heaven gate ascend,
> Bear on your wings and in your notes his praise;
> Ye that in waters glide, and ye that walk
> The earth, and stately tread, or lowly creep;
> Witness if I be silent, morn or even,
> To hill, or valley, fountain, or fresh shade
> Made vocal by my song, and taught his praise.
> (*PL* 5.171–172, 192–204)

As Adam and Eve hear it, every element of the natural world—animate or inanimate—makes continual music in praise of God. The winds are described as having musical dynamics, fountains and bodies of water carry "melodious murmurs," and all living souls are exhorted to join in a chorus of birds, fish, and animals of land. Even the landscape, "hill, or valley, fountain, or fresh shade," is given an echoing voice of praise, "made vocal by my song." Listening to the sounds of the natural world, Adam and Eve hear music expressing praise of the God who created that world.

In "At a Solemn Music," written some thirty years earlier, Milton had already described prelapsarian music as "the fair music that all creatures made / To their great Lord [...] whilst they stood / In first obedience, and their state of good" (ll. 21–24). At this point in his early poem, however, Milton intends the reader to understand prelapsarian music as strictly metaphoric—a figure for obedience to God. In his epic revision of the scene, the poet grandly literalizes his metaphor. In *Paradise Lost*, the hills—and winds and waters and creatures—are alive with the sound of music. This newly literal rendering of what he had before imagined only as metaphor suggests the growth of Milton's poetic sensibility, expressed through the prism of an epic vision in which spontaneous natural sounds occur in careful musical harmony.[9]

Adam and Eve enhance the music of the natural world. First, they exhort God's creatures to make music of praise; and second, their orison makes the landscape "vocal," so that the inanimate features of God's created world literally echo with song and, "taught his praise," figuratively express a relationship with God.

Even as their song affects the world, Adam and Eve are themselves affected by the celestial music they hear performed by angels. Earlier in *Paradise Lost*, the night before they sing their morning orison, Adam describes to Eve the angels' inspiring music:

> Millions of spiritual creatures walk the earth
> Unseen, both when we wake, and when we sleep:
> All these with ceaseless praise his works behold
> Both day and night: how often from the steep
> Of echoing hill or thicket have we heard
> Celestial voices to the midnight air,
> Sole, or responsive each to other's note
> Singing their great creator: oft in bands
> While they keep watch, or nightly rounding walk,
> With heavenly touch of instrumental sounds
> In full harmonic number joined, their songs
> Divide the night, and lift our thoughts to heaven.
> (*PL* 4.677–688)

This description specifies formal musical features: the "celestial voices" can be heard singing either solo or in a chorus—"responsive each to other's note," "oft in bands"[10]—and are often supported by an instrumental accompaniment that sets the songs with fully realized harmony. In Adam's account, the angels' music emerges as a detailed acoustic phenomenon. But it is also the natural expression of the "ceaseless praise" with which God's angels behold his works. To be God's creature means to behold his works with praise, which means, in turn, to sing of God as the *great creator*. By singing of God, the angels acknowledge their status as *creatures* of God. The angels' songs of praise, sonorously acoustic as they are, thus also represent their relationship with God.[11] The crucial effect of these songs, finally, is that, heard by Adam and Eve as both an acoustic phenomenon and a metaphoric expression of relationship with God, they "lift our [i.e., Adam's and Eve's] thoughts to heaven." Just as in "At a Solemn Music," heavenly music induces a "high-raised phantasy" ("At a Solemn Music" l. 5) in human beings and, in this state of heightened imaginative receptivity, inspires human rational minds to think of God.

Earlier still in *Paradise Lost*, Milton presents not a secondhand account of divine music, but rather the thing itself, as the angels in heaven praise the Son's intercession on behalf of humanity:

> [...] their golden harps they took,
> Harps ever tuned, that glittering by their side
> Like quivers hung, and with preamble sweet
> Of charming symphony they introduce
> Their sacred song, and waken raptures high;
> No voice exempt, no voice but well could join
> Melodious part, such concord is in heaven.
> (*PL* 3.365–371)

Unlike Adam and Eve's unaccompanied song, the angelic song is preceded by a sophisticated instrumental prelude. Yet if its sensuous, acoustic dimension is most immediately apparent, this music is nonetheless also metaphoric. With striking stylistic consistency, Milton uses a pun, just as he did in "At a Solemn Music," to signal acoustic–metaphoric duality. Both *symphony* and *concord* express two meanings. *Symphony* can signify a variety of musical concepts; the primary one, here, is probably "A passage for instruments alone [...] occurring in a vocal composition as an introduction, interlude, or close to an accompaniment" (*OED*, "music, *n*.5.a.").[12] But, in what is now an obsolete denotation probably derived from the word's Greek etymological root, *symphony* can also mean a nonmusical "agreement" or "accord" (*OED*, "symphony, *n*.3."). The *charming symphony* is thus at once an acoustic phenomenon—an instrumental prelude to song—and a metaphor for the unity of the angels.[13] This *symphony* has a specific purpose: to *waken raptures high*. Just as angelic music lifts Adam and Eve's thoughts to heaven, just as "At a Solemn Music" evokes the "high-raised phantasy" induced by music, so too does the angels' instrumental prelude *charm* the angels themselves into *high raptures*, a state of heightened feeling.

These raptures, in turn, impel each of them, "no voice exempt," to sing together in unified praise of God;[14] "such *concord* is in heaven," the epic narrator declares, introducing our second pun (emphasis added). Like *symphony*, *concord* can mean both a specific type of musical harmony—"A combination of notes which is in itself satisfactory to the ear, requiring no 'resolution' or following chord: opposed to *discord*" (*OED*, "concord, *n*.1.5.")—and the less obvious meaning: sociopolitical unity (*OED*, "concord, *n*.1.1.") . This pun identifies the music of the angelic choir as at once perfectly euphonious in sound, and also an expression of absolute unity with respect to the goodness of God and his Son. Inspired by their instrumental music, the angels' singing pays tribute to God both through its sonorous aesthetic beauty and as an act of unified obedience to God's monarchical power.

Music of praise is good music—beautiful, inspiring, unifying, and a sign of ethical awareness. Indeed, singing in praise is not just good; by reconciling material beauty with the moral duty to demonstrate absolute obedience to God, it is the best form of expression in God's universe. Taken as a whole, *Paradise Lost* suggests that music, more than poetry, is adequate to and necessary as an aesthetic vehicle for expressing the human indebtedness to God.

There is also bad music in God's universe. It expresses something rather different from indebtedness to God. The danger is that bad music does not *sound* bad:

> Others more mild,
> Retreated in a silent valley, sing
> With notes angelical to many a harp
> Their own heroic deeds and hapless fall
> By doom of battle; and complain that fate
> Free virtue should enthral to force or chance.
> Their song was partial, but the harmony
> (What could it less when spirits immortal sing?)
> Suspended hell, and took with ravishment
> The thronging audience. In discourse more sweet
> (For eloquence the soul, song charms the sense)
> Others apart sat on a hill retired.
> (*PL* 2.546–557)

The music-making of the fallen angels in Hell has lost none of the ravishing aural beauty of the music produced by faithful angels in heaven. In what ways, then—if any—does Milton establish a distinction between infernal music and divine music? Is it proper to speak of "good" and "bad" music in *Paradise Lost*? Or does Milton distinguish only between good and bad *musicians*?

One way to address the question is to focus on the distinction Milton draws between the music of a song and the text the song is setting. This is the approach taken by John Hollander, who locates the primary duality of Miltonic music in the binary form of "voice" (musical sound)

"Pure Concent": Music as Sound and Metaphor 47

and "verse" (text). Good music, Hollander argues, aligns a beautiful sound with a good text; by contrast, bad music ruptures such unity by combining a perverse text with a somehow still-heavenly sound:

> No matter what the perverse import of the text of the devils' epic song, the melody itself, partaking of the potency of the heavenly music, remains strongly effective. The notions of word and note are separated here in Hell; it is the doctrine which has suffered in the fall of the rebel angels, rather than the purely musical power to charm and move. But Milton carefully stipulates that it is the soul itself that is affected by the "rational" powers of "Eloquence," while "Song charms the Sense" alone and cannot, no matter how attractive, actually operate upon the highest psychic faculties. The philosophical discussions that are next described, although graceless, vagrant quests for the self-knowledge to which the fiends can never attain, must be "discourse more sweet," harmonious, and well attuned.
>
> (Hollander 318)

In Hollander's account, infernal music is "bad" because its text is bad, even while its sound remains angelic, still "charms the sense." That music made by angels—even fallen angels—cannot be sonically inharmonious indicates, for Hollander, that Milton believes "song" is naturally a lower form of expression than non-musical "eloquence," or rhetorically wrought language. On this account, music can appeal only to the sensual faculties, while eloquence always enjoys a higher appeal to the rational mind. Even though the fallen angels' "philosophical discussions" are self-serving, immoral sophistries, their "eloquence," Hollander asserts, is still better in Milton's eyes than their fallen song, which can never engage or inspire their rational faculties.

But since, as I hope to have shown, Milton elsewhere demonstrates a profound sense of music's abiding worth, I want to suggest an alternative way of reading the passage. This reading is suggested by a heavy irony in Milton's tone when he describes the actions and sensations of the fallen angels. This irony is difficult to ignore when one notices that the account of infernal music-making forms a striking textual parallel with the account of heavenly music-making examined above. I here juxtapose the two accounts, then list their parallel key terms:

Heavenly Music	Infernal Music
	Others more mild, Retreated in a silent valley, sing
Then crowned again their golden harps they took,	With notes angelical to many a harp
Harps ever tuned, that glittering by their side	Their own heroic deeds and hapless fall
Like quivers hung, and with preamble sweet	By doom of battle; and complain that fate
Of charming symphony they introduce	Free virtue should enthral to force or chance.
Their sacred song, and waken raptures high;	Their song was partial, but the harmony
No voice exempt, no voice but well could join	(What could it less when spirits immortal sing?)
Melodious part, such concord is in heaven.	Suspended hell, and took with ravishment
Thee Father first they sung omnipotent,	The thronging audience. In discourse more sweet
Immutable, immortal, infinite,	(For eloquence the soul, song charms the sense,)
Eternal king; thee author of all being.	Others apart sat on a hill retired.
(3.365–374)	(2.546–557)
Key Terms	**Key Terms**
1. *Nature of harmony*: "charming symphony," "concord"	1. *Nature of harmony*: "partial," "suspended"
2. *Performing forces*: "harps," "No voice exempt"	2. *Performing forces*: "many a harp," "others more mild," "partial"
3. *Effect of the music*: "waken raptures high"	3. *Effect of the music*: "took with ravishment," "charms"
4. *Purpose of the music*: "sacred"	4. *Purpose of the music*: "complain"
5. *Subject of the song*: "Thee Father first they sung omnipotent […] thee author of all being"	5. *Subject of the song*: "their own heroic deeds and hapless fall"

This juxtaposition clarifies what remains the same in the fallen, infernal music, and what is different. Like the good angels, the bad angels play harps; but where the music of the good angels is made by all the angels, participating together, in "concord," the music of the bad angels is sung by a select band of them, a group of "others more mild," in "partial" and "suspended" harmony. "Suspended" may be another musical pun; *suspension* is a technical term for the harmonic device in which an unresolved, dissonant harmony is maintained, or "suspended," before it is resolved by another, consonant chord.[15] But more important than a possible harmonic difference between good music and bad music are their definite differences in effect, purpose, and subject. Good angelic music serves to "waken raptures high," which galvanize the angels to sing a "sacred" song of God as the Creator. The bad angelic music, by contrast, in which the fallen angels sing a complaint about their own predicament, *takes* its audience *with ravishment*—a passive reception of carnal sensation that is itself the end effect of the song. Good angelic music first wakens rapture in all the angels, and then stimulates them into further music-making: the action of singing about God. By contrast, the bad angels first choose a subject—themselves and their woes—and then sing in order to give sensual pleasure to themselves and their passive, indolent audience.

With this contrast in mind, we can detect the irony in Milton's tone throughout the passage. That irony can be heard most clearly in the use, extended by zeugma, of the verb *charms*. The basis for Hollander's reading, in which music is merely sensual and thus inferior to the rational appeal of spoken language, is the narrator's parenthetical aside: "(For eloquence the soul, song charms the sense)" (2.556). But in this statement Milton is not affirming a general truth. Rather, his tone is ironic. For the fallen angels, the debased purpose of song is to give sensual pleasure, to *take with ravishment.* Its purpose, that is, is to "charm the sense." Here, *charm* means "to fascinate, captivate, bewitch, enchant, delight" (*OED*, "charm, v.1* 5.a."). Likewise, in the zeugma that extends the verb to apply also to *eloquence*, the purpose of debased infernal eloquence is to *charm*, or bewitch, the soul—an even sweeter pleasure for these angels whose souls are suffering the torments of Hell than the mere bewitching of their senses. Song and spoken eloquence are *both* corrupted by the angels' fall.

The word "charm" also occurs in the account of heavenly music. But there, it means something very different. Indeed, as he does throughout his epic, Milton registers the effects of the Fall semantically by presenting "fallen" and "unfallen" versions of a word. The crucial contrast between infernal and divine music hinges on this semantic bifurcation. In the fallen infernal world, *charm* means to captivate or enslave. In Heaven, by contrast, the unfallen angels produce "a preamble sweet of *charming* symphony" (3.367, emphasis added). As the "charming symphony [...] wakens raptures high," the word connotes another meaning altogether: "highly pleasing or delightful to the mind" (*OED* "charming, *adj.* 2.a.").

The contrasting uses of the word *charm* reveal the sharpest difference between infernal music and heavenly music. Contra Hollander, heavenly music, *charming* in that it is delightful to the mind, is indeed conducive to active rational thought for both angels and humans. Infernal music *charms*—bewitches, enslaves, and ultimately breaks down—active rational thought. Like an opiate, fallen music drowns its audience in indolent, passive, sensual pleasure. Hollander claims that "the notions of word and note are separated here in Hell" (Hollander 318). On the contrary, word and note are there unified in directing the fallen angels to think not of God, but rather of themselves.

The effect of the Fall is not, then, to rupture the fusion of text and notes, but rather to pervert music in its duality as acoustic phenomenon and metaphoric expression. As an acoustic phenomenon, infernal music charms the sense instead of stimulating rational thought; as a metaphor, it expresses not the unity of the heavenly host in obedience to God, but rather a splintering into individual self-serving indulgence. "Their song was *partial*," Milton carefully notes (emphasis added). Bad music is bad in the effect of its sound and in what it represents.[16]

Just as Satan's betrayal corrupts the ideal visual semantics of Milton's unfallen universe, in which the beauty of aesthetic form has a direct relation with goodness, so, too, does the Satanic fall corrupt the original correspondence between sonorous aesthetic beauty and moral duty. Bad music does indeed still generate a kind of aesthetic beauty, but this beauty does not raise our thoughts to heaven. Just the contrary. This observation leads to an urgent question: after the second fall, the fall of Adam and Eve, does all earthly music cease to reconcile aesthetic pleasure and Christian duty? Will music no longer raise human thoughts to heaven, but instead lower our thoughts to hell? In a fallen world, is all music infernal music?

Erin Minear argues that for the mature Milton, "Only in an unfallen world are nonverbal music and the poetic reverberation of such music right and safe" (16). Minear suggests that even prelapsarian music is suspect, registering Adam's inappropriately intense attraction to Eve (253). For Minear—and this is the central claim of her book on Shakespeare and Milton—Milton initially views music, which he associates with Shakespeare, as an exhilarating force that extends or disrupts the meaning of language; but later in his career, he comes to reject "Shakespeare's particular form of musical poetics" (1), viewing music as "a great temptation and a great danger" (3). The danger that Minear identifies, put perhaps too reductively, is that the sounds of music will disrupt its sense—and, by extension, threaten "a potential dissolution of moral meaning" (16). I argue the contrary, that it is indeed possible to produce moral music in a fallen world, and, further, that Milton considers it both possible and vitally important to listen to music with an ear attuned to its morality.

In the fallen secular world of *A Masque presented at Ludlow Castle, 1634*, appearances can be deceptive. A harmless shepherd turns out to be a sinister enchanter, and the heroine of the masque, the Lady, fails to discern his true identity until it is too late. If appearance can be manipulated to conceal true nature, how are the virtuous ever to judge the moral quality of people they encounter? The answer, Milton proposes, lies in music. In *Paradise Lost*, bad music sounds different from good music, and in its effect on listeners it behaves differently too. The contrast aids us in distinguishing between the badness of the fallen and the goodness of the faithful. But the reader is, of course, already aware that the Satanic crew is bad, the heavenly troops good; their contrasting musics heighten a known moral distinction. In the dark, morally uncertain "wild wood" of *A Masque*,[17] music serves as a crucial moral diagnostic feature—a sonic revelation of obscured moral identity.

When the Lady finds herself separated from her brothers, lost in the wood, she chooses to sing. This act is a rejection of passivity in the face of trial:

> I cannot hallo to my brothers, but
> Such noise as I can make to be heard farthest
> I'll venture, for my new-enlivened spirits
> Prompt me; and they [i.e., her brothers] perhaps are not far off.
>   *SONG.*
>
> (*A Masque* ll. 226–229)

The Lady characterizes singing as a kind of amplifying microphone for her voice, a sonic distress flare that, she hopes, will be noticed by her brothers as her merely spoken voice cannot be. But her song is more than that. Our primary account of the song comes from the kindly guiding spirit, who, disguised as Thyrsis, tells the Lady's brothers that he heard their sister's song from afar. "At last a soft and solemn-breathing sound," he says,

> Rose like a steam of rich distilled perfumes,
> And stole upon the air, that even Silence

> Was took ere she was ware, and wished she might
> Deny her nature, and be never more
> Still to be so displaced. I was all ear,
> And took in strains that might create a soul
> Under the ribs of death, but O ere long
> Too well I did perceive it was the voice
> Of my most honoured Lady, your dear sister.
> (A Masque 554–563)

This account of music first evokes song as a richly detailed acoustic phenomenon. Milton uses olfactory synesthesia, as the sound "[r]ose like a steam of rich distilled perfumes," to evoke both how the sound carries and the lush texture of the song. Next, a personification of Silence contrasts the music with the absence of sound, emphasizing the superior affective power of the former. The affective powers of music, as the Lady sings it, are capable even of endowing Death with a soul—that is, of giving a moral center to the demon *Paradise Lost* evokes as mortal enemy of humankind. "I was all ear," the disguised spirit declares, signaling, as if in summary, his concern with music as an acoustic phenomenon.

But the distinctive sound of the song—its aesthetic beauty and moral affective power—also serves a purpose beyond delighting the listener. It announces the identity of the singer: "O ere long," the spirit tells the brothers, "I did perceive it was the voice / Of my most honoured Lady." As the Lady had hoped, her song is heard from afar as *her* song; its distinctive acoustic qualities have served as an aural identification tag.[18]

Like the Lady's music, the music that Comus makes also reveals his true identity. Before he heard the Lady's song, the guiding spirit heard another musical production, one very different from the chaste music of the Lady. "I sat me down to watch upon a bank / With ivy canopied," the spirit tells the brothers, "[…] and began / Wrapped in a pleasing fit of melancholy / To meditate my rural minstrelsy" (542–543, 544–546). But even as he starts making some music of his own, the spirit is interrupted:

> but ere a close
> The wonted roar was up amidst the woods,
> And filled the air with barbarous dissonance.
> (A Masque 547–549)

This is bad music. Just as the Lady's song identified its singer as a virtuous woman, so too does Comus's dissonant music express his moral quality: *barbarity*.

The audience of the masque would have had a chance to compare Milton's diegetic descriptions of music with the real thing: performances of musical numbers by Henry Lawes. Five Lawes songs from *A Masque* survive, but we do not, alas, have any record of the music Lawes might have composed for Comus's "light fantastic round" (144). For a moment, let us imagine this music. We might expect a purely instrumental, rather than choral, setting, to allow for dancing, which would present a clear contrast with the vocal-and-instrumental music of the Lady (Lawes's lovely setting, "Sweet Echo," has remained a popular stand-alone song). But how would Lawes compose music that Comus calls a "light fantastic round" even as the spirit characterizes it as "barbarous dissonance?" A composer attuned to Milton's complex conception of music might write music that *sounds* engaging—harmonically consonant, rather than dissonant, and sprightly, in an energetic dance meter. Only when one examined more acutely would this music reveal its "bad" qualities: subtly off-balance rhythms, perhaps, or clumsy voice-leading, or inappropriate modulations. Whatever Lawes might have done, I suspect that Milton himself would have wanted his evil enchanter represented by music that seemed alluring, danceable, and charming, but with careful, active listening would reveal moral depravity.

When Milton has Thyrsis, the disguised spirit, characterize Comus's music as "barbarous dissonance," Thyrsis is not, I think, providing an assessment of the acoustic dimension of the music; rather, Milton is allowing our faithful spirit guide to help us distinguish bad music from good by describing its *metaphoric* dimension. Comus's music, as Milton describes it and as I imagine Lawes would have tried to compose it, is almost certainly not harmonically dissonant in any obvious way; rather, it is *morally* dissonant, expressive of carnal indulgence and hedonistic abandonment. Unlike his disguised appearance, however, which cannot be pierced by mortal eyes, Comus's music can—if carefully and actively listened to—reveal his true moral nature. As the Lady says, "This way the noise was, *if mine ear be true*, / My best guide now" (169–170, emphasis added). Emulating the guiding spirit, human beings must listen rigorously and ignore the sensual temptation of music. If our ear be true, it can be our best guide.

The Lady's song successfully announces her identity as a virtuous woman in contrast with the degenerate corruption expressed by Comus's music of orgiastic revelry. But although the spirit praises the Lady's song for its potential affective power—a sound "that *might* create a soul / Under the ribs of death" (emphasis added)—this song cannot in fact accomplish such action. The Lady's singing may reveal her moral identity, but it cannot ultimately transform bad into good. Comus hears the

Lady's music, and recognizes the moral identity of the singer—but he is not reformed:[19]

> Can any mortal mixture of earth's mould
> Breathe such divine enchanting ravishment?
> Sure something holy lodges in that breast [...]
> ....
> I have oft heard
> My mother Circe with the Sirens three,
> Amidst the flowry-kirtled Naiades
> Culling their potent herbs, and baleful drugs,
> Who as they sung, would take the prisoned soul,
> And lap it in Elysium, Scylla wept,
> And chid her barking waves into attention,
> And fell Charybdis murmured soft applause:
> Yet they in pleasing slumber lulled the sense,
> And in sweet madness robbed it of itself,
> But such a sacred, and home-felt delight,
> Such sober certainty of waking bliss
> I never heard till now. I'll speak to her
> And she shall be my queen.
> (*A Masque* 243–245, 251–264)

Comus gets it all right—and all wrong. He rightly recognizes the moral virtue of the singer, and detects the contrast between this song and the "sweet madness" of his own mother's drug-like singing, which, like the narcotics of "potent herbs, and baleful drugs," "lulled" its listeners into stupor. But although he recognizes the Lady as "holy," the pleasure Comus derives from her song is hardly moral. For him, the Lady's song is better than his mother's because it stimulates him into heightened sensual pleasure, delighting him with "waking bliss," that is, without putting him to sleep. This song is for him "enchanting ravishment"—Milton's word in *Paradise Lost*, some three decades later, for the passive sensual pleasure the fallen angels receive from their music. For Comus, the Lady's song is a new, better kind of aural opiate. Intoxicated by this drug, he resolves to make the Lady join him in his pursuit of voluptuous sensual pleasure: "I'll speak to her / And she shall be my queen."

Comus's response to the Lady's song shows us the limits of earthly music. For careful listeners, music can reveal the moral identity of its performers, but it does not accomplish any moral action on its own. Good music cannot reform moral corruption. Even worse, morally degenerate listeners are aroused by good music, taking it as a drug to heighten their debased pleasures.[20] The potential affective power of the Lady's song, its capacity to give Death a soul or to reform corruption, remains unrealized in the earthly realm.

At the close of the masque, however, Milton reveals that divine music, by contrast, can indeed accomplish action against the physical force of earthly evil. As the Lady remains stuck in Comus's "marble venomed seat" (915) even after the enchanter's defeat by the Lady's brothers, Sabrina "*descends*" and releases the Lady with the power of her heavenly song (920 [stage direction]). Introducing divine music into a fallen world, Sabrina realizes fully the potential affective power latent in the mortal Lady's song. Emanating from the divine Sabrina, music takes on an agency more efficacious against corruption than all the martial valor of the Lady's two brothers.

It is appropriate for Milton to develop the concept of music as a sonorous moral ID-tag in *A Masque*, rather than in *Paradise Lost*. *Paradise Lost* is an epic, while *A Masque* is a staged drama that includes diegetic musical performances. Although not himself the composer of the masque's musical numbers, Milton knew music would be integrated into the production of his masque. It has been remarked that in *A Masque* Milton revises features of the traditional courtly masque to render his drama a sort of "anti-masque" critiquing Caroline courtly culture.[21] This revisionary treatment extends to Milton's deployment of music in the masque. If musical numbers in Caroline masquing entertainments serve merely as aesthetically pleasing performances, for Milton, the music in a masque should not just give aesthetic pleasure but also stimulate the audience into a rational contemplation of moral qualities. In human fallen life, even if we cannot hope for the miraculous performance of divine music, Milton suggests that the music we do have can help us attain ethical clarity in a wild world of moral obscurity. If our ear be true, it can be our best guide.

There is no music in *Samson Agonistes*. This is a bleak, fallen world, as invisible to its readers—the work famously "never was intended" to the stage (Milton, "Of that sort of dramatic poem which is called tragedy")[22]—as it is to the blinded Samson. It is a world, moreover, of ethical obscurity, in which the defeated Samson struggles to focus on his role as God's chosen representative, champion of his people; in which the Chorus is even less ethically aware than Samson; in which the final catastrophe seems to provoke more ethical uncertainty than it resolves. The bleakness of this poetic vision has led critics, with Gordon Teskey, to deem it "Milton's strangest work" (Teskey, *Delirious Milton* 180). If *Samson Agonistes* stands apart from Milton's other large-scale poetic works, rejecting the aesthetic richness and moral clarity of *A Masque, Paradise Lost*, and *Paradise Regained*, it is only logical that Milton would also omit the clarifying aesthetics of music from his unstaged drama. In his earlier large-scale works, good music stands as the highest form of aesthetic achievement and the best means of expressing moral worthiness; just as important, the contrast between good and bad music helps both diegetic characters and Milton's readers to attain ethical clarity.[23] Music in its acoustic–metaphoric duality is central to Milton's poetic corpus because it unites aesthetics and ethics. That unity has no place in the aesthetically barren and ethically obscure world of *Samson Agonistes*.

Yet while he avoids music in *Samson*, Milton does not reject the acoustic–metaphoric potential of *sound*. The imagined stage of the closet drama is far from silent. In place of music, Milton gives us *noise*. At the close of the drama, as Manoa, Samson's father, tells the Chorus of Danites that he has had some success in negotiating with the Philistian leaders for the release of his son, the dialogue is suddenly interrupted:

MANOA
The rest was magnanimity to remit [in reference to the Philistines' retribution],
If some convenient ransom were proposed.
What noise or shout was that? It tore the sky.
(Samson Agonistes ll. 1470–1472)

Noise is not, here, that "melodious noise" of "At a Solemn Music." Nor is it even *dissonance*, which is, as an acoustic device, a specific component of an ordered harmonic system, and as a metaphor, an expression of moral badness.[24] No; *noise*, here, has no orderly aesthetic or metaphoric dimension whatsoever. It is, rather, the undifferentiated mixture of a number of different voices, not arranged via musical harmony into some coherent array—a chord either consonant or dissonant—but rather disarranged, in chaos: a cacophony.

Cacophony is not dissonance; it is, rather, the simultaneous sounding of many sounds at once such that there is a complete absence of musical order. The noise that interrupts Manoa is just that: a cacophony that has no aesthetic function and reveals no moral qualities. Its power lies in overwhelming intensity—"It tore the sky"—and its effect is to provoke uncertainty and conjecture. "Doubtless the people shouting to behold / Their once great dread, captive, and blind before them, / Or at some proof of strength before them shown" (1473–1475), the Chorus tells Manoa, trying to account for the cause of the noise. This surmise is in fact fairly accurate, but it is only a lucky guess, and it does not serve to restrain further incorrect conjecture by both the Chorus and Manoa.

Then comes the next noise, more abrupt and more terrible than the last:

> MANOA
> I know your friendly minds and—O what noise?
> Mercy of heaven what hideous noise was that?
> Horribly loud unlike the former shout.
> (*Samson Agonistes* 1508–1510)

Here is the climax of *Samson*: a deafening burst of cacophony that drowns out all speech. In that dash, "I know your friendly minds and—", Milton creates an anti-music, uncomposing the order of language, communication, even thought. But—and this is the crucial point—even here, the nature of sound is imagined as both acoustic and metaphoric.

The cacophonous climax of *Samson Agonistes* assaults the ear and unravels the power of language even as it enacts in sound the competition of jarring, incompatible ethical viewpoints articulated throughout the play: Samson's rage and desire to die; Manoa's well-intentioned desire to save his son's life at the cost of Samson's success as political leader; the partial truths and platitudes of the Danite Chorus; the self-serving politics of Dalila; the bellowing challenge of Harapha; the internal disagreement among the Philistian lords with respect to Samson ("Some much averse," "other more moderate seeming," "a third / More generous far and civil" [1461, 1464, 1466–1467]). Cacophony combines in a single, overpowering instant the narrative progression of Samson's *agon*. Indeed, the climactic instant of deafening noise forces us to recognize that the play, though it may dramatize some ethical progression in Samson's understanding of his role as God's hero, is finally also an unwinnable *agon* of incompatible voices—an ethical cacophony. It is that ethical cacophony, as much as the literal cacophony overwhelming the dramatic soundscape, that uncomposes any semblance of order in this play.

In the shocked aftermath of the hideous noise, Manoa, the Chorus, and the messenger attempt to shore up the fragments, to compose some new consonance, an ethically satisfying resolution to Samson's life. But their resolution fails to achieve a fully satisfying harmony. Manoa and the Chorus may write a euphonious history of the victors, but the play remains compromised by ethical and literal cacophony, submerged in meaningless sound.

If in *Samson Agonistes* Milton substitutes cacophony for music, depriving the dramatic world both of acoustic beauty and of real moral certainty, it is possible that he offers a compensatory gesture, however slight. In the front matter of *Samson* there appears a detailed note about the measure of the verse "used in the chorus":

> The measure of verse used in the chorus is of all sorts, called by the Greeks monostrophic, or rather apolelymenon, without regard had to strophe, antistrophe, or epode, which were a kind of stanzas framed only for the music, then used with the chorus that sung; not essential to the poem, and therefore not material; or being divided into stanzas of pauses, they may be called alloeostropha.
>
> ("Of that sort of dramatic poem which is called tragedy")[25]

Milton knew that in Greek tragedy the chorus did, in fact, sing, but he imagined it as a kind of semi-music, its poetry less carefully patterned than the strophic verse used in fully realized songs. Milton would most likely never have heard the very few fragments of ancient Greek music that survive today, and so the choral music of Greek tragedy would have remained for him a lost art, the ghostly echoes of an expired harmony. By invoking this ghostly music with the special measure of verse he uses for his chorus, Milton may have been gesturing towards the departure of music from his own poetic vision.

In *Paradise Lost*, Milton realized the musical model of "At a Solemn Music" on a grand stage, celebrating the song of praise as the highest aesthetic and ethical endeavor in God's universe. In *A Masque*, the poet had developed the capacity of music to distinguish between good and bad, and ultimately exulted in the potential for divine music to defeat earthly evil. In *Samson Agonistes*, the cacophonous thunderclap replaces Sabrina's divine song as the dramatic climax. Music no longer offers a harmonious resolution of aesthetics and morality, the material universe and the rational mind. Instead, noise conveys the aesthetically ravaged, ethically chaotic world of the play. Milton clings to the acoustic–metaphoric representational capacity of sound by attempting to use cacophony to represent ethical chaos. But cacophony, like chaos, is a tricky, horrid thing, resistant to aesthetic control. Once heard, cacophony is hard to unhear. In the thundercrack of Samson's final revenge, Milton, for once, allows the carefully designed architecture of his poetry to lose its intelligible shape, to fall into the disorder of moral ambiguity.

Notes

1. The *1645 Poems* has "content" rather than "concent"; "concent" appears in the *1673 Poems*. This is an intriguing variant tempting to interpret as a deliberate revision from representing a state of divine bliss (*content*) to representing the action required to achieve divine bliss (*concent*). Yet the publication and manuscript evidence suggest that "content" is simply a compositor's error. "Content" does not appear in any of the four versions of the poem included in the Trinity manuscript—which range from drafts to a fair copy—all of which have "concent." In addition, a copy of the *1645 Poems* in the Bodleian (8° M168 Art) presents a handwritten alteration, possibly Milton's own, Carey notes, of "content" to "concent" (see Carey's note to l. 6 of "At a Solemn Music").
2. The *OED* notes that in "early use," including the early modern period, *concent* and *consent* were "frequently confused." I am not suggesting that Milton was confused, but rather that he is deliberately drawing on the early modern propensity to interchange these homophonic words that are, in semantic terms, quite distinct (*OED*, "concent, *n*.").
3. In his reading of "At a Solemn Music," John Hollander also calls attention to "concent" as a pun, but finds the pun in two different *musical* senses: "celestial harmony" and "the agreement [...] of its own component elements, text and melody" (Hollander 328). Hollander is concerned with the relationship between text and music, rather than, as I am, with the dual nature of music as acoustic phenomenon and metaphor.
4. Past criticism of this poem has focused on its structure, generally finding it, as Pecheux has noted, to be divided into three or four sections (Pecheux 333). I concur with the division into three sections, but where past critics have found the poem's structure delineated by syntactic, cultural, or formal principles, I argue that it is the principally the interplay between the literal and the metaphorical that generates the poem's three-part structure. For a brief but exemplary syntactic reading of structure, see E. M. W. Tillyard, *Milton* (Macmillan, 1966), 56; for a somewhat abstruse cultural reading, see Leo Spitzer, "Classical and Christian Ideas of World Harmony: Prolegomena to an Interpretation of the Word 'Stimmung' (Part II)," *Traditio* 3: 307–364, esp. pp. 336–40; for a somewhat speculative formal reading based on the musical concept of the octave, see Mother M. Christopher Pecheux, "'At a Solemn Musick': Structure and Meaning," *Studies in Philology* 75.3: 331–46. Diane McColley's account, although filled with valuable insights, is distorted by the effort to interpret Milton's lyric poem by using analytical terms borrowed from music theory. See McColley, chapter 4: "'Sole, or responsive': voices in Milton's choirs," in *Poetry and Music in Seventeeth-Century England* (Cambridge, UK: Cambridge UP, 1997), 175–217.
5. Nor, it is interesting to note, is Milton concerned with the text of the song that the angels sing: while the poem opens with a plea for the sisters to wed *voice* and *verse*, the poetic emphasis is here on the *sound*, not the sense, of that unified music.

6 The Trinity manuscript, which includes four versions of "At a Solemn Music"—two initial drafts, a draft of ll. 17–28, and then a fair copy—presents a series of significant revisions to this section of the poem (see Carey's headnote, *Complete Shorter Poems*, p. 167). In particular, the characterization of the sound of human sin evolves from "harsh chromatic jars / Of sin" (first draft) to "harsh *chromatic* 'ill-sounding' jars / Of clamorous sin" (second draft), eventually becoming "disproportioned sin" in the third draft and fair copy (quoted in Carey's notes, "At a Solemn Music" l. 19n). Erin Minear points out that "Milton's revisions to the poem suggest a movement from the literal to the metaphoric [...]. Even if our response to heaven [in the first two drafts] is intended to be only metaphorically musical, the word 'chromatic' gives a very concrete sense of exactly what the jarring of sin would sound like" (Minear 194n71). Minear's reading of this poem aligns with my own insofar as she observes a shift from an initial literal sense of music to an "increasingly metaphorical" sense of music (193). But Minear identifies the "literal" aspect of music as principally "pictorial" rather than acoustic (193), and she does not observe the final turn to a redemptive hybrid acoustic–metaphorical model of music that I take to be the poem's climactic synthesis.

7 See Ainsworth, "Rapturous Milton and the Communal Harmony of Faith," *Milton Quarterly* 47.3, 149–162. Ainsworth's is a powerful argument for the intertwining of Christian theology and musical expression that accounts for Christian faith as the source of musicality. Erin Minear's reading of music in *Paradise Lost* is more closely related to my own in observing a representation of music "delicately suspended between the literal and the metaphorical" (Minear 250). But while Minear brilliantly detects in *Paradise Lost* a sonorous environment in which "[t]here is no real distinction [...] between literal and metaphoric music" (251), she also finds a tension or "danger" in this balance, a potential for "incursion of the literal on the figurative" (252). I argue, to the contrary, that Milton's representation of music as at once acoustic and figurative is never in and of itself a danger, but instead the very quality that makes music the most valuable aesthetic expression in God's universe. See Minear, chapter 7: "'Minims of Nature': Describing Music in *Paradise Lost*," especially pp. 250–53, in *Reverberating Song in Shakespeare and Milton*, 227–56.

8 The pun—a linguistic device that manipulates syntactic context to activate different semantic dimensions of a single word simultaneously—is a deft means of conveying the sense of two coincident dimensions coexisting within the same form.

9 In her account of the musical milieu of Paradise, Minear, too, briefly traces a connection between the figurative account of prelapsarian music in "At a Solemn Music" and the more literal representation of music in *Paradise Lost*. Minear observes this connection in passing, however, rather than considering and treating it at length, as I do here, as a central element of Milton's consistent yet also evolving model of music. Minear writes: "the world around [Adam and Eve] is full of wordless music, voiced and voiceless. The humans themselves are part of this music in all their words, all their

actions. One of the great achievements of *Paradise Lost* is to make this music more than metaphoric. Milton's language breathes the 'fair music that all creatures made' (*Solemn Musick*, 21) into life" (Minear 251). See chapter 7, *Reverberating Song in Shakespeare and Milton*, 227–56.

10 "Responsive each to other's note": this is probably an allusion to the *responsory*, in the Christian Church "A liturgical chant...said or sung by a cantor and choir alternately" (*OED*, "responsory, n.1.a."). If Milton does indeed intend "responsive" to evoke the ecclesiastical responsory, then he is imagining an unfallen, divine version of Church music in which each angel serves both as the cantor and the chorus—"responsive *each* to other's note" (emphasis added).

11 "Singing their great creator": Milton imports a Latinism by making "their great creator" the direct object of *singing*: the Latin verb *canere* (to sing) takes a direct object in the accusative case. Milton's imported Latinisms usually have a functional as well as an aesthetic purpose, and this one is no exception: the irregular, Latinate syntax emphasizes a thematic point. Unlike the opening line of *Paradise Lost*, where Milton exhorts the heavenly Muse to sing "Of," or *about*, "man's first disobedience and the fruit...," here, the angels are not taking "their great creator" as the *subject* of their song; rather, their song *directly* expresses the nature of God as their creator. In other words, it is a representation of their relation to God.

12 The two primary modern musical meanings—(1) a "(symphony) orchestra" or (2) a multimovement composition for orchestra—do not seem to have been active meanings of the word in Milton's era. The first meaning seems to have gained currency in the twentieth century, while the second entered popular usage in the late eighteenth century. Other musical denotations of *symphony* of which Milton would have been aware include: "Used [...] as a name for various musical instruments" (*OED*, "symphony, n.1."), "harmony of sound, esp. of musical sounds" ("*n.2.*"), and "Music in parts, sung or played by a number of performers with pleasing effect; concerted or harmonious music; a performance or strain of such music" ("*n.4.a.*").

13 The Greek etymology neatly registers the pun: symphony is *syn-* + *phônê*, together + sound (*OED*), i.e., "sounding together." The pun, referring at once to angelic unity and an acoustic phenomenon, thus captures the etymological senses of both "together" and "sound." I am grateful to Gordon Teskey for pointing out the meaning and Greek etymology of *symphony*.

14 For a discussion of the word *rapture* in the context of Milton's conception of music, see David Ainsworth, "Rapturous Milton and the Communal Harmony of Faith," *Milton Quarterly* 47.3, 149–162. Ainsworth argues that music causes the "communal experience" of rapture (149), which means that "Song and harmony thus stand in for, and can produce, Christian community and communion with God" (149).

15 The *OED* notes the first usage of "suspension" as a technical harmonic term only in the eighteenth century—still, some version of the word as a term of musical art may have existed in the seventeenth century, and Milton might then have known it. See chapter 1, n13.

16 Stephen Buhler offers a highly specific sense of how Milton intends to differentiate between the musical style of infernal and divine music. For Buhler, infernal music is polyphonic, divine music essentially homophonic. Buhler's reading hinges on the term "partial," which he argues means *polyphonic*—a style of music in which different melodic lines interact while maintaining overarching consonant harmony (Buhler, "Counterpoint and Controversy" 19). This passage of infernal music-making is key for Buhler in establishing Milton's position on a contemporary debate on the proper style of religious music. On Buhler's account, Puritans held that polyphonic music obscured the clarity of the sung text and so associated religious polyphony with high-church or Catholic excess. For Buhler, Milton codes polyphony—suspect in his own time—as fallen, a style associated with demons, while homophony is associated with divine, unfallen angelic music (18–20). Yet the contrast between divine and infernal angelic music may not divide quite so neatly on these stylistic lines. Diane McColley argues that Milton's divine angelic music "resembles the music of the English Church, the multichoral polyphony of the Roman one, and the *concertato* and *concertante* styles of Monteverdi" (McColley 206–207). For Buhler, heavenly music is "likely" homophonic, whereas for McColley, heavenly music is polyphonic. Who is right? Both, I argue, are too ready to correlate Milton's accounts of prelapsarian music with early modern musical practice. With music, as elsewhere in the epic, Milton imagines a complex prelapsarian aesthetics beyond fallen human comprehension. Thus, *pace* Buhler, while Milton is indeed distinguishing between the musical styles of the fallen angels and the loyal angels, I do not think that distinction inheres in the contrast between polyphony and homophony. *Partial* in this passage does not clearly mean "polyphonic" (it is not a listed denotation in the *OED*); polyphonic music is fundamentally consonant rather than dissonant, so, as Kerrigan, Rumrich, and Fallon point out in their edition of *Paradise Lost*, if "partial" meant "polyphonic," the fuller sentence—"Their song was partial, but the harmony [...] Suspended hell" (2.552-4)—would not really make sense: polyphony does offer harmony, not the absence of it (see Kerrigan, Rumrich, Fallon *PL* 2.552n, in *The Complete Poetry and Essential Prose of John Milton*, [Random House, 2007], 340). Rather, as McColley may start to suggest, Milton is imagining an angelic form of music in which, while the fallen angels do not attempt to collaborate in a deliberately polyphonic form, their individual songs nonetheless do not jar with one another—as though any angelic song, improvised and not designed to fit into another song, is somehow consonant with any other angelic song. One might indeed describe this effect as polyphony—the consonant interaction of independent melodic lines—but it seems instead to be a representation of an unimaginable angelic musical form in which harmony is achieved without premeditated recourse to any rules of counterpoint. This imaginary musical formal style expresses the communal ethics of the fallen angels. "Partial" is also, of course, a pun evoking the egotism of the demons, whose abiding interest is in personal contentment rather

than the welfare of the group—again in contrast with their unfallen peers. Just as they sing independently but somehow achieve a group harmony, the fallen angels are really self-serving but nonetheless achieve an infernal community.

17 "The first scene discovers a wild wood" (stage direction, Milton p. 178).
18 Minear reads this song in almost antithetical terms, as dazzlingly beautiful but ultimately dangerously *lacking* in precise identity: "The song, paradoxically, cannot fully express itself, neither in performance nor on the page" (202). For Minear, the song presents an aspirational but unrealized "wonder and holiness that remain highly desirable" (203), but ultimately, the song "retards forward movement" in the plot of the masque (202), typifying the "masque's treatment of the boundary between words and music as dangerously and excitingly *blurry*" (201, emphasis Minear's).
19 As Minear puts it, "though [the Lady's] song fills [Comus] with unfamiliar presentiments of holiness, it has little effect on his behavior" (202).
20 Minear offers a complementary reading, suggesting that Comus's account of the song actually magnifies its intended effect on the masque's audience: "Comus's description endows the Lady's music with a power that in itself, either in performance to an audience or read upon the page, it could hardly possess [...]. For the Lady's song to have its full effect upon *us*, we must believe that Comus's description—or at least some of it—is absolutely accurate. Indeed, the fact that such a wicked and depraved creature can recognize and enjoy the virtuous beauty of the Lady's song provides the best possible testimonial to its power" (209, emphasis Minear's). I recognize the powerful irony of giving Comus a "testimonial" to the power of the Lady's song but argue that Comus's partial recognition of the goodness in the Lady's song is ultimately outweighed by his sensual pleasure, which reduces the sound of moral good into an aphrodisiac.
21 For an introduction to the way in which *A Masque* is embedded in the political and cultural context of its day, see Leah Marcus, "John Milton's *Comus*," in *A Companion to Milton*, ed. Thomas N. Corns (Oxford, UK: Blackwell, 2001), 232–245.
22 In *Complete Shorter Poems*, edited by Carey, p. 357.
23 Within the compressed confines of its genre, *Paradise Regained* also accords music a crucial role: After Jesus has defeated Satan in the climactic tower temptation, a choir of angels sings of his triumph (4.593–637). This angelic chorus, praising God and Jesus, both clarifies the ethical import of Jesus's triumph and serves as the aesthetic resolution of *Paradise Regained*, rounding out the poem in glorious hymnal verse before a brief codetta recounts Jesus's return to his mother's home (4.636–639).
24 According to tonal music theory, a *dissonant* harmony must be followed by a *consonant* harmony that resolves it. Dissonance is subordinated to consonance and actually serves to *motivate* harmonic resolution. We have already seen in "At a Solemn Music" how Milton construes dissonance as a metaphor for sinfulness.
25 In *Complete Shorter Poems*, pp. 356–57.

Part II
Milton in Music

3 Handel's Cacophony

Samson, Noise, and the Right to Music

To turn from poetry to music requires a precise object of inquiry—a specific topic connecting a poetic work to a musical adaptation of it. In this chapter, I take up the topic of cacophony in *Samson Agonistes* and George Frideric Handel's musical adaptation of it, *Samson*.

In Part I of this book, we have seen that Milton's poetic engagement with music represents a rich strand of his intellectual development. Writing about music in his poetry pushed Milton towards his mature monist materialism, even as it allowed him to balance between superlative aesthetic beauty and rigorous moral duty. By the end of his career, Milton was even able to take the risk of representing the dangerous phenomenon of cacophony in his poetic verse. But with this dangerous phenomenon, we come to a pointed version of a larger question that the first part of the book as a whole raises. Is Milton's concept of music in poetry—as a material phenomenon, at once acoustical and metaphorical—purely theoretical? Or can it be realized in actual music? The more specific, indeed extreme, version of this question that I consider in this chapter is whether real music can express Milton's concept of *cacophony*.

Before the twentieth century, the very idea would have been dangerously transgressive. Modernist composers, chiefly Igor Stravinsky and Arnold Schoenberg, paved the way for experiments in post-tonal dissonance, but prior to modernism, noise was by and large considered the very opposite of music, a perceived threat to notions of aesthetic order. Throughout the Baroque, Classical, and Romantic periods, to be accused of cacophony was to be accused of an assault on music itself. Yet it is precisely the demand to represent cacophony that would have been confronted by Handel, one of the leading Baroque composers, when he decided to create an oratorio based on Milton's *Samson Agonistes*. As we considered in the previous chapter, when Milton's Samson drags down the temple of Dagon, the poet allows the untrammeled force of

DOI: 10.4324/9781003378389-6

cacophony to enter his dramatic soundworld—a precarious moment, not only for the play, but also for Milton's larger poetic project. While cacophony might seem to be assimilable to Milton's poetic model for music—this "hideous noise," acoustically anguished, seems also to function metaphorically by capturing in sound the discordant ethical world of the play—cacophony is the antithesis of order, and thus resistant to aesthetic representation. To attempt to represent cacophony is to invite disorder.

If it is so for literature, how much more so for music? After all, Milton is writing a closet drama, not for the stage, "to which this work never was intended" (Milton, "Of that sort of poem which is called tragedy").[1] In *Samson Agonistes*, cacophony—like music in Milton's earlier poetry—must be imagined by the reader, not expressed in real sound. For a composer of actual music, however, some musical sound must be found to simulate or suggest the disorder of cacophony, that simultaneous sounding of multiple voices in complete disagreement. Yet if it seems that literature has it relatively easy when it comes to cacophony, Milton raises the stakes higher than we might expect. The poet courts aesthetic disorder not only by dramatizing a cacophonous moment, but also in the strange, elliptical manner in which he chooses to dramatize it. Before considering how Handel confronts the problem of representing cacophony in music, let us consider in closer detail how Milton himself confronts it as a matter of formal poetic representation. How does the poet insert the quantity of noise into the metric confines of his verse play?

We return to the climactic scene of *Samson Agonistes*. Samson has gone offstage to the temple of Dagon. Left behind are Samson's father, Manoa, and the Chorus, who talk together about the possibility of winning Samson's freedom from the Philistines by paying them ransom. In the midst of their conversation, they hear a strange noise:

MANOA
The rest was magnanimity to remit,
If some convenient ransom were proposed.
What noise or shout was that? It tore the sky.
    (*Samson Agonistes* ll. 1470–1473)

The noise or shout in question occurs after an end-stopped line, in a convenient place, where the reader naturally pauses. It is evidently loud and disorderly, but not cataclysmic. The Chorus assures Manoa that it is just the crowd jeering at Samson, or maybe cheering for him. The conversation resumes for a few dozen lines; all seems well; in fact, even the elsewhere metrically variable Chorus conforms to a strict iambic pentameter:

> CHORUS
> Thy hopes are not ill founded nor seem vain
> Of his delivery, and thy joy thereon
> Conceived, agreeable to a father's love,
> In both which we, as next, participate.
> *(Samson Agonistes* 1504–1507)

Manoa responds, or tries to:

> MANOA
> I know your friendly minds and—O what noise?
> *(Samson Agonistes* 1508)

Here the noise is cataclysmic—even apocalyptic: "Horribly loud unlike the former shout," declares the shaken Manoa, and the Chorus agrees: "Noise call you it or universal groan / As if the whole inhabitation perished, / Blood, death, and deathful deeds are in that noise, / Ruin, destruction at the utmost point" (1510–1514). Apocalyptic, yet finally unexplained—and because unexplained, even more terrible. Only later, when the Messenger arrives, is the "universal groan" explained as the destruction of the temple of Dagon and the shrieks of those crushed within it.

I have discussed the nature of this noise, the "universal groan" of cacophony, in Chapter 2. Here, I am less interested in the noise itself than in what the noise does to the line that contains—or tries to contain—it. Here is the line with its metric stresses emphasized:

> I **know** your **friend**ly **minds** and—**O** what **noise**?

The offstage noise breaks into Manoa's speech and forces him to stop. After the noise ceases, Manoa begins anew. The violent climax of Milton's drama occurs in that break. What happens to the meter of the line? The line shudders to a halt as the offstage climax occurs, yet in its prosody it is still a perfect iambic pentameter line: ten syllables, patterned in remarkably even accentual iambs.[2]

In the tension between a caesura that violently "breaks" the line and a perfect iambic pentameter line as a whole, I want to argue that Milton allows the reader a radical freedom in determining the poetic meter. It is the *reader* of the closet drama playing out in the reader's mind who must imagine the offstage noise and its duration. By locating the climax of his play in a pause, Milton rejects, however temporarily, the formal principle of meter. Only the reader's imagination determines the length of the climactic pause. As the reader's imagination enters the line, meter loses all measure. It is a moment of subjectivity wherein the poet cedes control to the reader. Yet when the reader resumes reading the line, meter reasserts itself, containing the moment of imagined climax. And so Milton contains the subjective freedom of the reader's imagination within the perfectly regular objective structure of the line.

The line offers a formal mimesis of Samson's predicament: the struggle to fit the subjectivity of a singular, suffering individual into the rigid, unconforming objectivity of a reality that marches on despite the individual's pain. Within this paradigm, the reader's imagination forms an analogy with Samson, while the perfectly metric line enacts historical reality. Trying to interpret the line is as problematic as trying to interpret the play: does Samson's individuality triumph—does the reader's imagination delay the line inevitably?—or does reality—that is, meter—reassert itself? If the inevitable answer is that the play must go on, and so meter must win out, nonetheless, the force of the reader's imagination leaves an irreducible trace in the line.

The broken line brings to a climax Milton's career-long experimentation with meter. It combines the extraordinary metric skill of the versifier of *Paradise Lost* with a radical willingness to allow the reader's imagination equal responsibility in propelling—or suspending—the line.[3] Throughout his career, Milton's distinctive prosodic technique had been founded in exceptionally strong metric beats that give his pentameter lines—most notably in *Paradise Lost*—a propulsive thrust quite unlike the prosody of any other poet.[4] Yet Milton's most daring experiment with meter occurs when he delays the thrust of a line, breaking it in two, and it is no accident that this breakage occurs in a line that attempts to imagine—by not explicitly representing—cacophony. If music is for Milton a material phenomenon that is represented in poetry as at once figurative and real, metaphor and acoustical event, then the antithesis of music, cacophony, *requires* an aesthetic breakage—a material lacuna—in the poetic medium itself. This is a caesura that carries a great deal of weight. Music pushes Milton's imagination towards an aesthetic monism in which the material phenomenon of sound resonates acoustically and ethically; cacophonous noise can be captured in the poetic model, but only just barely—and the act of capturing cacophony distends and breaks the formal medium of poetry itself.

We are now in a position to turn to Handel's setting of the climax of *Samson Agonistes*. How will the Baroque composer, operating under the strict rules of tonal harmony and within a culture that privileges consonance and beauty, render cacophony in music? Handel's 1743 oratorio, titled simply *Samson*, with libretto by Newburgh Hamilton, is in three acts. The offstage climax takes place in Act 3. Hamilton closely follows Milton, with two offstage noises, the first intensely loud, the second climactic. After Samson has left the stage to perform at the temple of Dagon, Manoa enters to speak with Micah, who is Hamilton's adaptation of Milton's Hebrew Chorus. As in Milton's play, Handel's Manoa hopes to win the freedom of Samson and strikes up a conversation with Micah:

MICAH
Old Manoa, with youthful steps, makes haste
To find his son, or bring us some glad news.

MANOA
I come, my brethren, not to seek my son,
Who at the feast does play before the Lords;
But give you part with me, what hopes I have
To work his liberty.
(Hamilton and Handel 3.2)[5]

At this point, Manoa is interrupted. Milton's version is largely the same: Manoa speaks at greater length about the possibility of ransoming Samson (Milton ll. 1457–1471), but then an offstage noise interrupts him. Milton's reader, like Manoa and the Chorus, does not immediately know the cause of that noise: "What noise or shout was that? It tore the sky," says Milton's Manoa (Milton 1472), and the Chorus responds "Doubtless the people shouting to behold / Their once great dread" (Milton 1473–1474). In Hamilton's libretto, any ambiguity as to the nature of this first offstage noise is fully removed, for the librettist provides first an aria sung by a Philistine man, and then an accompanying choral number sung by the Chorus of Philistines:

MANOA
But give you part with me, what hopes I have
To work his liberty.

(Air and Chorus of Philistines at a distance.)

72 *Milton in Music*

PHILISTINE
Great Dagon has subdued our foe,
And brought their boasted hero low:
Sound out his [i.e., Dagon's] pow'r in notes divine,
Praise him with mirth, high cheer and wine!

CHORUS OF PHILISTINES
Great Dagon has subdued our foe,
And brought their boasted hero low:
Sound out his [i.e., Dagon's] pow'r in notes divine,
Praise him with mirth, high cheer and wine!
                            (Hamilton and Handel 3.2)

After the aria and chorale setting, Manoa sings to Micah, "What noise of joy was that? It tore the sky" (Hamilton and Handel 3.2). Where Milton leaves the offstage noise only suggested, requiring the reader to imagine its particularities, Handel fully realizes this noise as an actual event in the musical drama. And where Milton suggests the offstage noise is frighteningly intense, some indistinguishable roar of cacophony, Handel's musical setting smooths and civilizes the tearing noise into a decorous aria and chorus (see Example 3.1).

Example 3.1 "Great Dagon has subdued our foe"
(Handel p. 232, systems 1–2)

Handel's Cacophony: Samson, Noise, and the Right to Music 73

In Handel's setting, first a Philistine man and then the Chorus of Philistines sing a solemn celebration of their triumph and the triumph of their god. The choral number follows directly out of the aria and is essentially a four-part harmonization of the aria. While the text refers to jubilation and drinking, Handel's setting is, at least outwardly, characterized by dignity, delicacy, and restraint. Set in a refined E minor that modulates into G major for understatedly joyful stretches, the setting scarcely strikes the listener as a raucous celebration that "tore the sky."

Perhaps the only musical characterization of sybaritic excess is provided by a sinuous melisma, or florid melodic embellishment of a single syllable of text, on the word "wine," which suggests drunkenness (see Example 3.2):

Example 3.2 Drunken melisma
(Handel p. 234, system 3, m. 10; p. 235, system 1, mm. 1–4)

Still, for sky-tearing riotousness, this is rather tame.

At first hearing, the next, climactic instance of cacophony is no more promising as music of violent discord. As the climax approaches, Hamilton's libretto follows Milton exactly. Manoa is speaking to Micah when he is suddenly interrupted:

MANOA
I know your friendly minds, and…
(Hamilton and Handel 3.2)

Just as in Milton's drama, Manoa is interrupted mid-sentence. But unlike in Milton's play, where the line is "broken" only by the reader's imagination as it conjures up cacophony, in Handel's oratorio, the composer fills in the blank by composing actual music to convey the offstage noise. Here, then, is the challenge of cacophony confronted head-on. How does Handel do it? First, he writes a *sinfonia*, or instrumental interlude—what the libretto calls a "symphony of horror and confusion" (Hamilton and Handel 3.2 [stage direction]). To what extent is the music in fact expressive of "horror and confusion?"

Handel mimetically conveys the suddenness of the interruption by directing the orchestra to begin playing their "symphony of horror and confusion" on an upbeat just after Manoa sings the word "and" (see Example 3.3). As the orchestra's upbeat follows Manoa's last note *attacca* (without pause), Handel neatly captures the abruptness of the offstage commotion. The effect is striking both on the page and in musical performance. Typically, Handel inserts a double bar line at the end of a recitative, or section of sung dialogue advancing the plot of an opera or oratorio, indicating formal closure both in a symbolic sense, on the page, as well as the practical possibility for the performing forces to pause as long as they wish before beginning the next musical number. Here, however, the recitative runs directly into the following sinfonia, so that on the page, the sinfonia appears to be a continuation or interruption of the recitative, while in performance, the musicians are urged to continue without pause.[6] Handel is trying to startle the audience.

Example 3.3 Manoa is interrupted by a "symphony of horror and confusion" (Handel p. 247, system 1, mm. 4–5; system 2, mm.1–3)

But while the rhythmic onset of the symphonic interlude surprises the audience with abrupt suddenness, Handel's harmonic progression effects a smooth transition between Manoa's recitative and the orchestral number. Before Manoa sings, the key signature is a clear A minor, as Micah sings to Manoa, "Your hopes of his deliv'ry seem not vain, / In all which Israel's friends participate" (Hamilton and Handel 3.2). As Micah sings his second line, Handel makes a fairly routine modulation from A minor into the relative major, C major; the transition from the minor to the major mode, with its characteristic brightening sound, suggests the hopeful sentiment of Samson's "deliv'ry." Yet at the close of Micah's phrase, the continuo unexpectedly cadences not in C major, but instead in the parallel minor, C minor. It is a strange

Handel's Cacophony: Samson, Noise, and the Right to Music 75

moment: the harmonic backdrop seems to act independently from the singer's melodic line, which could easily be set over a C-major harmony. Why C minor, with its dark and brooding affect? The libretto does not imply that Micah's sentiment suddenly changes from optimism to pessimism; is Handel embedding a character cue in his harmony, suggesting that Micah's mood abruptly changes, although his words do not convey such a change? The confusion grows. When Manoa responds to Micah, the strange, harmonically wayward C-minor cadence is revealed not to be the tonic, or home key, but rather a harmonic transition into a new home key: G minor (see Example 3.4).[7] The harmony makes sense on its own terms, but dramatically, why should Manoa, who is responding with gratitude to Micah's optimistic statement, move into the darkly solemn region of G minor? The harmony seems to be disagreeing with the sentiment of the singer. Only the ensuing sinfonia finally elucidates this strange tension.

Example 3.4 Micah speaks with Manoa
(Handel pg. 247, system 1, mm. 1–5)

The "symphony of horror and confusion" is set in G minor. Thus, we realize, the entire harmonic sequence underpinning the exchange between Micah and Manoa is designed to modulate from A minor, the initial key signature, into the G minor of the sinfonia. The more straightforward interpretation is that Handel decided his "symphony of horror and confusion" should be set in G minor, a key he likely understood as conveying grimness or despair. Once he made his decision, Handel had to modulate expediently from A minor, a distant harmonic region, into G minor; to do so, the composer effects a clever harmonic transition beneath the recitative sung by Micah and Manoa. On this account, Handel sacrifices a convincing dramatic characterization of Micah and Manoa on the altar of harmonic expediency.

An alternative interpretation, attending to the representational possibilities of the orchestra, offers a more subtle rationale for Handel's use of harmony. In a musical scenario that combines voices and orchestral accompaniment, the orchestra can mean many things. It might represent the dramatic background, in the sense of either physical setting or of the scene's mood; the internal emotion of the singers; thematic elements in the sung text; physical objects that appear on stage; or any combination of these elements. While the use of the orchestra became ever more complex and nuanced as opera developed into the nineteenth century, Baroque composers such as Bach and Handel were skilled at deploying the orchestra to convey an intricate range of emotions, themes, and physical settings.[8]

If it is clear that in the symphonic interlude Handel uses the orchestra to convey the noise of Samson's destruction of the temple, how should we interpret the orchestral continuo that precedes the interlude? Handel is not only preparing the audience for a musical event that is to come, but also, more subtly, suggesting that offstage activity is already occurring. While Micah and Manoa speak optimistically of Samson's delivery, the audience is made aware, via the minor mode harmony, of Samson's imminent demise. More subtly, Handel uses the continuo part, usually relegated to the role of harmonic backdrop for recitative, to simulate in music an additional dramatic dimension—the offstage action that is occurring simultaneously with the onstage action.[9] Handel fashions a complex species of dramatic irony that uses shifting harmonies in the orchestra to suggest dramatic action that is not directly represented in the text.

Even so, the music that follows does not, when considered in strictly mimetic terms, seem adequately to convey the "horror and confusion" specified in the libretto. Even allowing for Baroque harmonic conventions, Handel would not seem to make any bold effort to defy convention. The composer instead adopts stock techniques connoting violence or emotional turbulence: a key signature in the minor mode, a headlong tempo (*presto*), and chromatic inflections (see Example 3.3, system 2, measure 3). The final movement of Vivaldi's *Summer* concerto, from the ubiquitous *Four Seasons* (written some twenty years before *Samson*, ca. 1720), uses similar musical gestures to whip up a far greater sense of violence.

After the sinfonia, which at twelve measures lasts scarcely twenty seconds, Manoa sings a recitative in reaction to the intruding noise: "Heav'n! What noise! / Horribly loud, unlike the former shout" (Hamilton and Handel 3.2). At this point in Milton's play, the Chorus and Manoa continue to describe the quality of the "hideous noise" without being quite certain what has occurred; their uncertainty only adds to the terror of the moment. But once again, Hamilton and Handel depart from their source to alleviate the terrifying ambiguity

Handel's Cacophony: Samson, Noise, and the Right to Music   77

of the cacophonic noise. As soon as Manoa finishes his recitative, a further offstage "noise" occurs: the Philistines sing a chorus as the temple collapses around them (see Example 3.5):

Example 3.5 The Philistines lament their demise as the Temple of Dagon falls (Handel p. 248, sys. 1–2)

> Hear us, our God! oh hear our cry!
> Death! ruin! fall'n! no help is nigh,
> Oh mercy, Heav'n! we sink, we die!
>   (Hamilton and Handel 3.2)

This setting is a choral version of the "symphony of confusion and horror" that the orchestra had played only a few seconds before. Although the text gives the Philistines a despairing death cry, the musical setting is again generated out of stock techniques, failing to find some fresh or convincingly mimetic expression of violent discord. Does Handel then avoid any special effort to render the sounds of cacophony in music?

Simply to fault Handel for not making cacophonous music, however, is reductive. Bound by Baroque conventions, Handel was also writing an oratorio for polite English society.[10] Even had the composer been capable of conceiving it, outright dissonance was hardly the thing to appeal to such an audience. Considered in thematic rather than purely aesthetic terms, however, Handel's rendering of Milton's cacophony in fact provides a striking display of artistic originality. While Handel does not appear to invent any radically new formal means to convey the extreme nature of cacophony, he accords the cacophonous offstage events a special status within the thematic structure of his oratorio. That structure is rather different from Milton's original. Handel and his librettist, Newbugh Hamilton, make sweeping changes to their source material, turning Milton's stark, sparsely populated homage to Greek drama into a refulgent, bustling Baroque oratorio. For Milton, *Samson Agonistes* is a personal drama, centered on the *agon*, or heroic struggle, of its protagonist. For Handel and Hamilton, however, *Samson* is a communal drama, centered on a clash between cultures. It is in this cultural clash that cacophony will play a decisive role.[11]

The *Agonistes* of Milton's title, derived from the Greek *agon*, or contest, presents Samson as "contestant" in verbal and psychological battles with a procession of foes (Carey 349);[12] the final combat takes place within Samson himself, as he must come to terms with his diminished status and decide how best to fulfill his role as God's elected hero. Hamilton and Handel drop the term "*Agonistes*" from their title. While they include Samson's series of "contests," their focus widens to take in both the Hebrew culture of which Samson is the heroic representative, as well as the culture against which the Hebrews have continually struggled. Milton represents the Hebrew people through the stock Greek figure of the chorus. While the Greek chorus was sung by a group of people, the poetry of the chorus is a collective voice expressed in the play script as a single character. In Milton's closet drama reimagination of Greek tragedy, which lacks a musical score and does not require casting, the Chorus of Danites functions as a single, first-person-plural character.[13]

With the need to provide music for a genuine musical chorus, Handel and Hamilton revise Milton's single collective voice into a musical group—a chorus in the modern literal musical sense of the word.[14] But beyond the theatrical expediency of including a chorus, Handel and Hamilton take the further step of introducing a second chorus, the Chorus of the Philistines. The inclusion of two choruses drastically alters the terms of the drama. Every scene of the three-act, over three-hour-long oratorio is marked by choral involvement, and the drama itself plays out as nothing less than a spiritual battle between the two competing cultures that the choruses represent.[15] This cultural battle takes place not in a direct, military confrontation, but rather through the proxy of a somewhat unexpected, if also entirely appropriate, aesthetic battlefield: music.[16]

In *Samson Agonistes*, as we have seen in the previous chapter, Milton leaves out music altogether. In *Samson*, Handel makes music-making a central feature of the plot. Milton's drama opens with a self-flagellating speech by the remorseful, blinded Samson:

> A little onward lend thy guiding hand
> To these dark steps, a little further on;
> . . . .
> Light the prime work of God to me is extinct,
> And all her various objects of delight
> Annulled, which might in part my grief have eased,
> Inferior to the vilest now become
> Of man or worm; the vilest here excel me,
> They creep, yet see, I dark in light exposed
> To daily fraud, contempt, abuse and wrong [...]
> . . . .
> O dark, dark, dark, amid the blaze of noon,
> Irrecoverably dark, total eclipse
> Without all hope of day!
>   (Milton ll. 1–2, 70–76, 80–82)

Samson's self-excoriating lament extends over one hundred lines before the Hebrew Chorus hesitantly intrudes on his anguished solitude. The opening of the drama firmly establishes the despairing Samson as its dominant figure. From this "total eclipse" of his personal hopes, can Samson come to terms with his reversals, gain a new measure of understanding, and renew his sense of responsibility as God's hero? This is the central question on which Milton constructs his drama.

By contrast, after an opening orchestral overture, Handel's Samson only sings a few lines before he is interrupted not by the Hebrews, but by a group of Philistines:

> SAMSON
> This day, a solemn feast to Dagon held,
> Relieves me from my task of servile toil;
> Unwillingly their superstition yields
> This rest, to breathe heaven's air, fresh blowing, pure and sweet.
>
> CHORUS OF PHILISTINES
> Awake the trumpet's lofty sound!
> The joyful sacred festival comes round,
> When Dagon king of all the earth is crown'd.
> (Hamilton and Handel 1.1)

The contrast between Handel's opening scene and Milton's could not be more pronounced. Instead of Milton's Samson's unremitting lament, Handel's Philistines take over the scene with an extended celebration of their holy day in celebration of their god, Dagon. They celebrate with diegetic music—that is, music actually made within the world of the musical drama: "Awake the trumpet's lofty sound!" cries the Chorus of Philistines, associating the ascendant power of their god with triumphal music-making:

> PHILISTINE WOMAN
> Ye men of Gaza, hither bring
> The merry pipe and pleasing string,
> The solemn hymn, and cheerful song;
> Be Dagon prais'd by ev'ry tongue!
>
> [The Chorus of Philistines repeats their setting of "Awake the trumpet's lofty sound!"]
>
> PHILISTINE MAN
> Loud as the thunder's awful voice,
> In notes of triumph, notes of praise,
> So high great Dagon's name we'll raise:
> That heav'n and earth may hear how we rejoice!
> (Hamilton and Handel 1.1)

For the Philistines, music-making is both an act of praise and a declaration of totalizing power. They aim to make their triumphal music

Handel's Cacophony: Samson, Noise, and the Right to Music 81

as loud as thunder, to convey Dagon's superiority throughout "heav'n and earth." This is a literal claim that their triumphal music-making will echo throughout an expansive physical realm. But it is also a symbolic claim that, drawing on the cultural prestige of music-making, the Philistines can stake out Dagon's full dominion over both the temporal and the spiritual domains of human life.

Handel renders the Philistines' claims for music in musical settings that emphasize sonic intensity, triumphal pomp, and a cohesive communal identity (see Example 3.6):

Example 3.6 The Philistines' triumphal invocation of music (Handel pg. 11, system 1, mm. 1–3, system 2, mm 1–4)

As the oratorio unfolds, the Philistines, politically and culturally ascendant, continually invoke and make music. Like Milton in *A Masque*, Handel uses music as an ethical barometer of the music-maker. What does the music-making of the Philistines reveal? Triumphalism, as we have seen, but also hedonism:[17]

> CHORUS OF PHILISTINES
> To song and dance we give the day,
> Which shows thy [i.e., Dagon's] universal sway.
> . . . .
> Sound out his pow'r in notes divine,
> Praise him with mirth, high cheer and wine!
> (Hamilton and Handel 2.4, 3.2)

To pay homage to Dagon, for the Philistines, means to indulge in a drunken day of "song and dance." Through Handel's careful dramaturgy, the Philistines' music-making expresses their character. But with a bold matching of his artistic medium with the thematic content of the drama, Handel also uses music-making as a means of identifying political power. The right to music is the emblem and insignia of political power in the world of *Samson*.

The subjugated Hebrews do not make music.[18] Their chief concern, in servitude, is to present an unshaken faith in the Hebrew God. Hamilton and Handel do not elect to allow the Hebrews to express their faith through music-making. Instead, the Hebrew Chorus invokes the sober, unassailable authority of the Bible:

> Oh first created beam! and thou great word:
>   "Let there be light!"–and light was over all;
> . . . .
> Then round about the starry throne
> Of Him who ever rules alone,
> Your heav'nly-guided soul shall climb:
>   Of all this earthly grossness quit,
>   With glory crown'd for ever sit,
> And triumph over Death, and thee, oh Time!
>   (Hamilton and Handel 1.2, 1.3)[19]

In expressing their faith to God, the Hebrew Chorus does not call on the celebratory power of music. Instead, Hamilton and Handel symbolize the Hebrews' disempowered political status by refusing them the right to make music within the drama. Disenfranchised, if not wholly broken, the Hebrew people speak but do not sound "notes divine"; they have no power—as do the Philistine people—to "awake the trumpet's lofty sound."

Handel's oratorio is, then, a clash of cultures fought in the arena of music. Whoever has the right to make music has political power. Before Samson's death, the right to music is accorded solely to the Philistines. After Samson's death, everything changes. With Samson's slaughter of the Philistines, the Hebrews gain what is in effect a military victory, and the balance of political power shifts. Handel recognizes this shift in power by giving the Hebrews the right to music. By the close of the oratorio, the Philistines have not only lost the right to music but also the power of utterance altogether. The Hebrews, by contrast, first use the power of music to memorialize Samson, and then appropriate fully the power of music as a triumphal emblem of cultural ascendancy.

It is within the narrative of this shift of musical power that offstage cacophony turns out to have climactic significance. Consider the two offstage "noises"—first, the joyful noise of Philistine celebration, and second, the ruinous noise of the temple's destruction—in light of the transfer of musical agency from the Philistines to the Hebrews. The first noise, we recall, expresses the Philistines' essential character: a sybaritic intertwining of music with drunkenness (see Example 3.2). During the occurrence of the second noise, which Handel splits into two separate acoustic events—first the "symphony of horror and confusion," followed shortly thereafter by a choral setting—the Philistines are robbed of the power to make music ever again.

This is obviously true in a literal sense—the Philistines are killed and so deprived of the power not only to make music but to do anything at all—but Handel derives symbolic meaning from this literal event. Here, at last, is the composer's distinctive solution to representing cacophony within a musical stylistic idiom that refuses rampant dissonance: Handel construes cacophony as the *loss of the power to make music*. If cacophony is, literally, a vertical harmonic event—the discordant simultaneous sounding of multiple voices in complete disagreement—then Handel translates it into a horizontal, narrative event occurring over time: the climactic loss of the right to music.

In this light, Handel's choral setting offers a powerful formal rendering of the loss of musical voice. First, Handel inserts his "symphony of horror and confusion," which serves as an introduction to the following chorus and provides the musical material for that choral setting. Then, after Manoa's shocked interjection, the Philistines express their despair in a prayer to their god, Dagon, imploring his intervention. As we saw, the musical setting offers no mimesis of death or destruction. It is, however, ingeniously designed to symbolize the loss of musical voice. Rather than having the Philistines sing together in a homophonic, or rhythmically unified, outcry, Handel chooses to employ points of imitation, or staggered entrances, in which first one section of the chorus, say the basses, sings a motif, and then that motif is repeated in sequence by the other sections (see Example 3.5, mm. 3–5). One effect of deploying this musical texture at this climactic instant is that the hegemonic musical unity of the Philistines is symbolically broken. An even more powerful effect derives from how Handel sets the Philistines' singing within the orchestral backdrop. As the Philistines sing their fragmented vocal lines, the orchestra does not imitate their melodic formulas, but instead plays rhythmically and melodically distinctive material musically at odds with the singing it ostensibly accompanies. If the musical backdrop—in its stylized rather than mimetic fashion—stands in for the destruction of the temple, then Handel suggests that the voices of the Philistines are swallowed up by those sounds of destruction, even as they express the desire to be heard by their god. The power of music to raise up Dagon's name so it is heard in both "heav'n and earth" (1.1), which the Philistines earlier proudly celebrated, is now definitively reversed. Both in the literal sense of sound and in the symbolic sense of cultural ascendency, the Philistines can no longer make Dagon's name heard. Milton's "hideous noise," the line-breaking cacophony of his closet drama, is reconfigured as the loss of the right to music; cacophony is rendered not as a mimetic phenomenon but as a symbolic narrative event.

After the Philistines' right to music is swallowed by the orchestra in a moment of Handelian cacophony, the diegetic sonic space—the soundworld Handel imagines within the world of his drama—becomes available for the Hebrew people to fill with music. Micah declares that the Hebrews will honor Samson's body with "great acts enroll'd / In verse heroic, or *sweet lyric song*" (Hamilton and Handel 3.3, emphasis added). In the closing moments of the oratorio, an Israelite woman sings a song less lyric than triumphal:

> ISRAELITE WOMAN
> Let the bright Seraphim in burning row,
> Their loud, uplifted angel-trumpets blow.
> Let the Cherubic host, in tuneful choirs,
> Touch their immortal harps with golden wires.
> (Hamilton and Handel 3.3)

Ellen T. Harris suggests that "the lively rejoicing" of this aria "can feel unseemly, not just in terms of Samson's self-inflicted death but also the deaths of the Philistines" (298). Harris notes further that the Israelite woman's aria was not at first included in the oratorio, which "originally ended with the requiem for Samson [...] [T]he joyful coda was added before the first performance, probably to satisfy audience expectations" (Harris 298). Handel was an astute caterer to audience pleasure, but I would suggest that the Israelite woman's song is more than a concession to popular taste. As the Israelite people reclaim cultural ascendency, Handel closes the oratorio by staking out their right to music. That this right is being appropriated from the Philistines is made quite clear by the libretto. The trumpet, symbol of Philistine music-making from the opening of the oratorio—"Awake the trumpet's lofty sound!" (1.1)—has now been claimed by the Hebrew people. Handel cannily recognizes this appropriation in his musical setting. "Let the bright seraphim" is a dazzling showpiece for coloratura soprano and trumpeter that revels, with a kind of competitive collaboration, in the twinned virtuosic potential of the human voice and the musical instrument. With trumpet and voice raising the name of their God throughout heaven and earth, the Hebrew people have seized both the sign and the sound of the right to music.

The text for the aria is itself a striking act of appropriation. Hamilton lifts these lines from Milton's early lyric, "At a Solemn Music":

> [...] the bright seraphim in burning row
> Their loud uplifted angel trumpets blow,
> And the cherubic host in thousand choirs
> Touch their immortal harps of golden wires.
>   ("At a Solemn Music," ll. 10–14)

It is no accident, I think, that to celebrate the final triumph of Hebrew music-making Handel and Hamilton turn from the stark world of Milton's *Samson Agonistes*, bereft as it is of music, to Milton's brilliant early enunciation of music's divine power. For it is in this poem, as I have argued earlier in this book, that Milton first articulates his distinctive poetic model for music and makes his strongest claim for its salvific efficacy.

Why have Handel and his librettist departed so sharply from Milton's vision of *Samson Agonistes* to fashion a world resounding with diegetic music, in which the central conflict of the drama concerns the right to music as a touchstone of cultural power? Diegetic music-making has an inherent fascination for composers, and in the nineteenth century, opera composers demonstrated considerable ingenuity in distinguishing between the texture of their musical medium and inset music made within their dramatic worlds.[20] By contrast, Handel deploys diegetic music to fashion within his drama an allegory for the proper use of music. If the cultural conflict between the Hebrews and the Philistines plays out as a battle for the right to music, then for the Christian Handel, writing, as he was, for a Christian audience, the final victory of the Hebrews represents the triumph of the music of divinity over the music of blasphemy.[21] In this sense, *Samson* not only dramatizes the victory of the music of divinity, but also, ultimately, justifies its own non-diegetic music-making.

Rather than attempting to render cacophony as iconoclastic dissonance, Handel obeys Baroque convention to realize cacophony thematically as a reversal of the right to music. To compare Handel's formal rendering of cacophony to Milton's is instructive. Milton engages in a boldly original moment of formal experimentation by "breaking" his line. Handel does not "break" his form. Instead, as he uses the overarching narrative structure of his oratorio to reclassify cacophony not as a literal event but as a thematic idea, the composer deploys more subtle formal devices—the fragmentation of choral unity and the swallowing-up by the orchestra of the fragmented chorus—to suggest the nature of his thematic representation of cacophony. Milton recognizes the extreme ontological status of cacophony by breaking his form; Handel brackets the extreme ontological status of cacophony through formal ingenuity.

Handel's rendering of cacophony might seem in these terms an evasion of artistic danger, a retreat from the challenge of representing pure noise. Indeed, Handel's musical idiom, its Baroque elegance and consonance, may not itself strike the modern audience as particularly well suited to adapting Milton's unforgiving late style. In addition to bringing music into a world that Milton had imagined as bereft of music, Handel's oratorio offers a sleeking-over of Milton's rough, challenging prophetic verse into a smoothly efficient Baroque entertainment. Yet the stylistic incongruity would seem to be deliberate. Elsewhere, in the remarkable oratorio *L'Allegro, il Penseroso ed il Moderato*, Handel conjures up a soundworld profoundly attuned to Miltonic lyric style.[22] In *Samson*, however, we have a fine example of a composer repurposing Milton's text in the service of a rather different imaginative vision. As personal drama becomes communal conflict, the queasy, restive ethical uncertainties of Milton's unsettling tragedy are resolved in a burst of grandly confident spiritual clarity.

Handel's rendering of cacophony also poses a rigorous challenge to Milton's poetic theory of music. For Milton, music is a material phenomenon that both sounds and, through its sound, produces metaphorical meaning. In its material combination of acoustics and metaphor, music serves as a perfectly mimetic art in which form expresses moral meaning. To listen acutely to music, in the Miltonic cosmos both prelapsarian and post-, to attend to it with the Lady's "true" ear (*A Masque*, l. 169), is to engage with its ethical content. For Handel, however, at least in *Samson*, the sound of music cannot be inherently mimetic of its ethical or even thematic content: cacophony is unrepresentable, and by extension, musical sound itself cannot be understood as inherently metaphorical.

Is this implicit objection to Milton's poetic theory of music decisive, or is it particular to Handel's musical values, embedded as they are within the tonal strictures of eighteenth-century harmony? Handel's rendering of *Samson Agonistes* suggests that Milton's demanding theory of music may have been impracticable not only in the eighteenth century but in Milton's own time—that within the consonant dictates of Renaissance and Baroque harmony, Milton's thinking on music was more visionary than practical.

Post-tonal music, however, affords new options. In my final chapter, I turn to the twentieth-century composer Krzystof Penderecki. Enfranchised by the post-tonal harmony of the mid-twentieth century, Penderecki composes an iconoclastic opera of *Paradise Lost* that indeed successfully realizes Milton's theoretical ideal for monist music as at once acoustic phenomenon and powerful metaphor.

But the last word, at least in this chapter, should go to Handel. If the Baroque composer transforms the apocalyptic quality of Milton's stark drama into society entertainment, the composer closes his work by returning to Milton's early lyric vision of the transformative power of heavenly music. Milton would almost certainly have objected to this injection of radiance into Samson's darkness. But while Handel disagrees with Milton on the purpose and character of Samson's story, the two artists ultimately align in their final understanding of divine music as a transcendent vessel of goodness in a hopelessly fallen world.

Notes

1 In *Complete Shorter Poems*, edited by Carey, p. 357.
2 David Ainsworth suggested in reviewing this book in manuscript that one might consider the final foot a spondee: **what noise**. But this possibility scarcely abrogates the prevailingly iambic meter of the line.
3 For an overview of lineation in *Paradise Lost*, see John Creaser, "The Line in *Paradise Lost*," in *The Cambridge Companion to Paradise Lost*, ed. Louis Schwartz (Cambridge: Cambridge UP, 2014), 81–93.

4 For a magisterial account of iambic pentameter in Shakespeare with some attention to Milton, see George T. Wright, *Shakespeare's Metrical Art* (Berkeley and Los Angeles: U California P, 1988).
5 I have used the convention of Act #.Scene # for citation—e.g., Act 3, Scene 2 = 3.2. Line numbers are not provided in my copies of the libretto. Although the libretto is by Hamilton and is listed as such in my works cited, I cite quotations as "Hamilton and Handel" to avoid ambiguity. All references to the libretto of *Samson* are to the edition edited by Friedrich Chrysander. All musical examples are also drawn from this score, which is in the public domain and available online at imslp.org: https://imslp.org/wiki/Special:ImagefromIndex/18755/hfal. The libretto may also be found in the booklet notes for the recording of Samson conducted by Harry Christophers (Coro, 2002).
6 Indeed, following Harry Christophers' brilliant idea on his recording of the oratorio, one might even take Handel's scoring as an implicit invitation to play the orchestral eighth-note upbeat not after but rather simultaneously with Manoa's final eighth-note (Disc 3, Track 13, 0:16–0:17). This performing decision makes the interruption literal.
7 Handel prepares the modulation: the C-minor cadence is in the first inversion, indicating it is not likely to be the tonic, and is instead probably going to serve as a predominant harmony. Indeed, in the following measure, a D-major dominant seventh chord (in first inversion) followed by a G-minor triad in root position complete one of the basic harmonic progressions to confirm a tonic key: $IV^6-V^{6/5}-I$.
8 A high point in the development of the orchestra as producing complex meaning is reached in Richard Wagner's pioneering of the leitmotif. For the leitmotif and its development in the twentieth century, see Matthew Bribitzer-Stull, *Understanding the Leitmotif: From Wagner to Hollywood Film Music* (Cambridge, UK: Cambridge UP, 2015).
9 Strictly speaking, none of the action of an oratorio—essentially an unstaged opera sung in concert—is staged. Nonetheless, it is still proper to make a distinction between "onstage" and "offstage" action, referring to the activity that is so specified by the libretto. Similarly, it is proper to distinguish between onstage and offstage action in Milton's closet drama.
10 For an account of Handel's life and art while living in England, see Ellen T. Harris, *George Frideric Handel: A Life with Friends* (New York: Norton, 2014). For an account of Handel's collaborative work with librettists to prepare *Samson* (as well as his other major Milton-based oratorio, *L'Allegro, il Penseroso ed il Moderato*), see Ruth Smith, "Milton Modulated for Handel's Music," in *Milton in the Long Restoration*, edited by Blair Hoxby and Ann Baynes Coiro (Oxford, UK: Oxford UP, 2016), 159–177.
11 For an account of Handel and Hamilton's work in altering Milton's original to produce the libretto for their oratorio, see Ruth Smith, "Milton Modulated for Handel's Music," in *Milton in the Long Restoration*, edited by Blair Hoxby and Ann Baynes Coiro (Oxford, UK: Oxford UP, 2016), 159–177.

12 See both *OED*, "agon, *n.*" and "agonistes, *adj.*," and Carey's note on the title of *Samson Agonistes* in the *Complete Shorter Poems*, p. 349.
13 At the close of his drama, Milton does divide his chorus into two halves, or *Semichoruses*, but even here, the two halves each speak collectively. In at least one modern partial staging of this closet drama, I saw the chorus played by a single actor.
14 The *OED's* first instance of "chorus" as a group of singers is from 1656 (*OED*, "chorus, *n.*3.a."). Ruth Smith notes usefully that "The roles of the Israelite Chorus, and of its quasi-leader Micah, correspond to two aspects of practice and theory in the contemporary drama: to the taste for 'sympathising woe', and to early and mid-eighteenth-century advocacy for the revival of the chorus, particularly as an agent of sympathy with the protagonist and as a guide through the moral maze" (Smith, "Milton Modulated" 173).
15 Smith, too, recognizes how the libretto confers on the Hebrews a larger societal identity than does Milton's play: "The Chorus of Samson's friends is not tribal but national: not fellow-Danites but a group of Israelites [...]. The hero of [Handel's] oratorio is at least as much the nation as Samson" (Smith, "Milton Modulated" 172, 173). Smith briefly considers the potential resonance Handel's oratorio would have had with contemporary British political causes (174). What Smith refers to as the political unit of the *nation*, I describe as the anthropological unit of *culture*; and where she is concerned with teasing out potential political resonance connecting the oratorio with the British nation, I am concerned with the internal cultural conflict of the oratorio.
16 While critics such as Anthony Hicks have noted that Handel captures the differing character of the Philistines and the Hebrews through the "contrasting styles of [their] choral music," I am instead concerned with diegetic music-making—the music made within the reality of the drama. See Hicks, booklet notes for *Samson* (Coro, 2002), p. 4.
17 Hicks, too, notes that Handel uses the style of the Philistines' choral music to portray them as a "hedonistic race" (Hicks 4).
18 This is not, of course, to say they do not sing in the performance of the oratorio. The distinction is once again between diegetic music, music made within the reality of the drama, and non-diegetic music, music understood as a feature of the dramatic medium. The Hebrew Chorus does not make *diegetic* music—they do not make music within the reality of the drama. As an audience outside the dramatic work, we understand their *non-diegetic* singing as the nature of utterance in a musical drama such as an oratorio.
19 This second excerpt is one example of Hamilton's borrowing from other works by Milton—these lines are an adaptation of the final lines of Milton's early lyric, "On Time" (ll. 17–22). For a full list of all the Milton works from which Hamilton borrowed in *Samson*, see Ruth Smith's "Milton Modulated for Handel's Music," Table 8.1 (Smith 161).
20 Two striking examples of diegetic music-making are Verdi's setting of Desdemona's "Willow Song" in *Otello* and Lakmé's Bell Song in Delibes'

Lakmé. For a seminal account of the Bell Song, see Carolyn Abbate, "Music's Voices," in *Unsung Voices: Opera and Musical Narrative in the Nineteenth Century* (Princeton: Princeton UP, 1991), 3–29.

21 This evident theological judgment may not be incompatible with human sympathy for the costs of genocidal violence. Harris suggests that in his portrayal of the Philistines and elsewhere in his musical dramas, "Handel's settings also display a deep sympathy for all victims, at the very least in the portrayal of their suffering [...]. When Samson brings down the temple of Dagon on himself and his foes, the crushing of the Philistines is set by Handel in a harrowing chorus" (Harris 298). See this book's conclusion for a consideration of Handel's surprising cultural empathy for the Philistines.

22 For their part, Milton's companion poems offer famously beguiling accounts of music, but these accounts reveal that the poet has not yet worked out the analytical model of music first articulated in "At a Solemn Music." See the conclusion of this book for a consideration of how Handel's *L'Allegro, il Penseroso ed il Moderato* helps identify the limits of Milton's thinking about music in the companion poems. For an account of the development of the libretto for *L'Allegro, il Penseroso ed il Moderato*, see Ruth Smith, "Milton Modulated for Handel's Music," especially pp. 160–168.

4 Making a Hell of Heaven and Earth

Music as Sound and Metaphor in Penderecki's *Paradise Lost*

With its treatment of cacophony, Handel's *Samson* rebukes Milton's poetic theory of music as more visionary than practical. The twentieth-century composer Krzysztof Penderecki, however, finds a way to realize that theory in actual musical sound. If the larger mimetic latitude of post-tonal music, its capacity for abrasive noise, might make such success seem logical or even inevitable, Penderecki's distinctive achievement is to draw on postmodernist harmony to capture not the cacophony of *Samson Agonistes* but the prelapsarian world of *Paradise Lost*.

Joining a select few composers to take on Milton's epic, Penderecki writes an iconoclastic, abrasive opera, one that presents such a challenge to performers and audience that it has never entered the standard repertory. All the more a shame. Penderecki's expressionistic style in this opera is the vehicle for a musical philosophy of quite remarkable nuance, one that ultimately not only realizes Milton's own theory but also offers an interpretive lens on Milton's poem that illuminates the surprising optimism of the original epic.[1] Penderecki holds out hope for human redemption, and like Milton thinks music is the best way to achieve such redemption, but his vision of human experience, even prelapsarian experience, emerges in a fractured soundworld of bewildering dissonance.

The bewilderment begins with the opera's first curtain. After a spoken introduction to the opera, what we see and hear first is not the aftermath of Satan's fall—where Milton begins the action—but rather the aftermath of the fall of Adam and Eve:

ADAM
O fleeting joys of Paradise
Dear bought with lasting woes!
. . . .

(*EVE comes to him and ADAM turns on her in disgust*)

ADAM
Out of my sight,
Thou Serpent!
That name best befits thee
Thyself as false and hateful.
But for thee I had persisted happy.

EVE
Impute thee to my default that
Which might have happened to thyself
Had thou been there?

ADAM
Would you had harkened to my words,
And stayed with me.
               (Fry and Penderecki p. 5)[2]

How different is our first encounter with Penderecki's Adam and Eve than our first encounter with Milton's. For Milton, Adam and Eve enter the epic in the proud station of heroic innocence: "Two of far nobler shape erect and tall, / Godlike erect, with native honour clad / In naked majesty seemed lords of all" (4.288–290). Unlike the animals around them, the unfallen Adam and Eve stand physically and morally upright.

Penderecki's Adam and Eve enter the opera not "Godlike erect" but abject, fallen past the point of moral no return. The striking decision to open the opera after the human fall is key to the thematic structure of the opera. Yet critics both literary and musical have not attributed any real importance to the opening scene. On the literary side, P. G. Stanwood dismisses the opening as merely an "anticipation of all that will follow in the course of the opera" (Stanwood para. 12); on the musicological side, Regina Chłopicka argues more compellingly that the composer's intent in beginning with the human fall is to focus attention on Adam and Eve and their "internal transformations and experiences" (Chłopicka 147). I would go rather further: by beginning after Adam and Eve have committed original sin, Penderecki sets the entirety of the ensuing drama in the condition of human fallenness. Everything that occurs—even if it occurs in a flashback to before the fall, as does much of the action—occurs under the shadow of the human fall.[3]

There are dramaturgical as well as thematic consequences to beginning the opera at the end of Book 9 of Milton's epic. Milton's plot must be reordered. Penderecki and his librettist, Christopher Fry, alter the plot to emphasize the pervasive condition of fallenness. After the opera begins with the fracturing of marital unity, Fry and Penderecki bring us back to the beginning of Milton's poem: the crash landing of Satan and his crew in Hell. Thereafter, the opera unfolds as an extended flashback, drawing ever closer to the narrative moment with which it opens. Only midway through Act II do we reach that moment and proceed past it, into what Milton presents as Books 9–12. Once the initial extended flashback begins, the opera in fact pursues a more linear chronology of events than Milton's more temporally complex narrative. As Stanwood notes, the "rearrangement of episodes in Fry-Penderecki seems justified [...] in terms of their wish to make an obviously coherent drama that moves from beginning to end in a largely sequential way" (Stanwood para. 12). As a result of putting events in something like a strictly linear chronological order, the setting, at least initially, shifts back and forth between Hell and Earth more frequently than does Milton's poem. The juxtaposition suggests a moral equivalence between Earth and Hell (see Table 4.1).[4]

Table 4.1 Plot sequence in Penderecki's *Paradise Lost*

Event	Location
Act 1	
[The character of Milton presents an invocation (Fry and Penderecki p. 5)]	[UNSPECIFIED]
1. The newly fallen Adam and Eve quarrel (p. 5)	EARTH (EDEN)
2. Satan and the fallen angels convene their infernal council (pp. 6–7)	HELL
3. The Creation of Man (7)	EARTH
4. Satan resolves to seek out Man and journeys out of Hell into Chaos (7–9)	HELL
5. Adam names the animals and Eve is created (9)	EARTH (EDEN)
6. Satan's speech on Mt. Niphates (10)	EARTH (EDEN)
7. Eve and Adam meet, court, and marry (10)	EARTH (EDEN)
8. Satan observes Adam and Eve's marital consummation, overhears their discussion of the forbidden fruit, and resolves to make them fall (10–11)	EARTH (EDEN)
9. Satan causes Eve to dream of disobedience, is arrested by angelic guards, and flees a confrontation with Gabriel after an adverse celestial sign (11–12)	EARTH (EDEN)

(*continued*)

Table 4.1 Cont.

Event	Location
10. Eve recounts her troubling dream to Adam (12)	EARTH (EDEN)
11. God's voice commands Raphael to warn Adam (12)	[NO CHANGE SPECIFIED; "*the light of God*" appears (12)]
12. Raphael visits Adam and Eve (12)	EARTH (EDEN)
13. Eve wins Adam's permission to work apart from him until noon (12–13)	EARTH (EDEN)
Act 2	
[The character of Milton gives a narrative invocation (13)]	[UNSPECIFIED]
1. Satan, disguised as the serpent, tempts Eve; Eve falls (13–14)	EARTH (EDEN)
2. Eve brings Adam the fruit and he falls (14–15)	EARTH (EDEN)
3. Adam and Eve enjoy their fallenness in "love's disport" (16)	EARTH (EDEN)
4. Sin and Death build a bridge over Chaos from Hell to Earth, then, gloating, meet Satan, who sends them down to Paradise (16)	HELL, CHAOS, EARTH
5. Adam and Eve awaken, lament their fallenness, and cover themselves with fig leaves (16–17)	EARTH (EDEN)
6. As Sin gloats, Messias (the Son of God)[5] appears and volunteers to sacrifice himself so that Man may live (17)	[NO CHANGE SPECIFIED; "*the light of God*" fills the stage (17)]
7. God's Voice judges Adam and Eve while Messias observes (18)	EARTH (EDEN)
8. Adam and Eve pray in contrition (18)	EARTH (EDEN)
9. Messias returns to Heaven and intercedes with God on Man's behalf (18)	HEAVEN
10. Satan returns to acclaim in Hell; all the fallen angels are transformed into snakes (18–19)	HELL
11. Adam and Eve see signs of the Fall and are visited by Michael, who presents to Adam a vision of the future (19–22)	EARTH (EDEN)
12. Adam and Eve are expelled from Paradise (22)	EARTH (EDEN)

After the initial oscillation between Earth and Hell, the action settles in Eden and remains there throughout the remainder of the opera, save for some brief excursions to Hell, Chaos, and Heaven. Heaven's near absence from the opera presents one of the most striking differences between the operatic scenario and its epic source.

Music as Sound and Metaphor in Penderecki's Paradise Lost   95

While musicological criticism of the opera has tended to emphasize how Penderecki differentiates among the worlds of God, humanity, and Satan, the libretto in fact only once specifies Heaven as a spatial location.[6] The critical events that occur in Milton's Heaven are left out of the libretto almost entirely. Gone is most of the dialogue between God and the Son; entirely absent is Raphael's narration to Adam of the war in Heaven and the creation of the world.[7] The opera thus focuses obsessively on the lower planes of existence: Earth and Hell. In its representation of these spatial realms and the social order within them, Penderecki's *Paradise Lost* contracts and lowers Milton's vast cosmology. Opening with the human fall and confined to a diminished universe, the libretto provides the composer with a dramatic vehicle centered on fallenness.

Adam and Eve's opening duet establishes the thematic and stylistic parameters for an opera of fallenness (see Example 4.1). Penderecki's music slyly subverts traditional operatic expectations. In the eighteenth and nineteenth centuries, when two or more singers sing together, their rhythms and harmonies characteristically align, even if they are violently disagreeing.[8]

Penderecki, however, never allows Adam and Eve to sing "together." When Adam rounds on Eve to denounce her, exclaiming, "But for thee I had persisted happy" (Fry and Penderecki 1), Eve interrupts Adam before he can finish (Score: Example 4.1, system 1, measure 1; recording: Act 1, part 1, 07:22 ff.).[9] But even as she tries to sing over Adam, Eve enters the opera on a weak upbeat, or unaccented beat preceding the strong downbeat, at the end of a short measure in 3/4 time that is substituted for the prevailing 4/4 time signature. With her entrance tucked in at the end of a measure and out of rhythmic alignment with the orchestra's downbeats, Eve's vocal line is off balance. Penderecki invites the singer to sing Eve's opening—notated *piano*, or quiet—with stumbling uncertainty.

Even after she interrupts him, Eve's vocal line remains suggestively out of alignment with Adam's. Eve defends herself against Adam's accusation that she is to blame for his fall—"Impute thee to my default that / Which might have happened to thyself / Had thou been there?" she protests (Fry and Pendrecki 1)—but Adam does not wait for her to complete her phrase. He resumes singing as Eve articulates the words "my default" (Example 4.1.1.3): "Would you had harkened to my words," Adam cries (Fry and Penderecki 1). While before Adam's singing had aligned with the downbeats in the orchestra, his angry retort now begins on an upbeat, and Eve's singing, in contrast, begins to harness the orchestral downbeats. "Impute thee to *my* default," she sings

Example 4.1 Adam and Eve quarrel
(Penderecki p. 16, systems 1–2)

© 1978 SCHOTT MUSIC, Mainz–Germany. Reproduced by permission. All rights reserved.

(Example 4.1.1.3; emphasis added), enlisting the orchestral downbeat on the personal pronoun to stress her indignation at Adam's accusation. As they bicker, the couple's rhythms, too, are completely out of phase. Whenever Eve sings in triplets, Adam sings in eighth-notes; as soon as Eve starts singing in an eighth-note based rhythm, Adam switches over to triplets. The effect is not so much of concerted polyrhythm—when two different rhythms are articulated simultaneously to create a complex interaction—as of confused disunity. As far as their rhythms go, Adam and Eve simply cannot agree.

Nor can they agree on their singing style. After Eve's appearance, Adam insistently focuses on the pitches of B and C; his vocal line emerges as a declamatory reciting tone, indebted both to *recitative*, the speech-based singing style used for dialogue and plot advancement in traditional opera, and to the earlier *stile concitato* of Renaissance Italian music, in which repeated pitches figure a throbbing emotion.[10] Adam wants to remain on B or on C; Eve, by contrast, enters on a falling half-step, from A♭ down to G, and her first phrase hesitantly descends in a chromatic scale. This phrasal contour is an allusion to the *lamento* topos, a melodic figure traditionally associated with intense grief.[11] Where the *stile concitato* is a mimetic style of expression evoking the sounds of intense emotion, the dignified *lamento* figure is metonymic rather than mimetic, a symbol rather than the sound of grief. As they enter the opera, Adam and Eve belong to different and incompatible stylistic worlds.

Riven apart in rhythm and style, Adam and Eve belong, finally, to different worlds of tonality. Adam's insistent pitches are B and C; when Adam interrupts Eve to demand, "Would you had harkened to my words,"[12] he articulates a hectoring C (Example 4.1.1.3). Meanwhile, however, Eve is singing a G♭. The interval they describe is a diminished fifth—in modern tuning, equivalent to the tritone.[13] A dissonance that retains the power to shock even in post-tonal contemporary music, the tritone was traditionally known as the *diabolus in musica*, "the devil in music." Regina Chłopicka notes that in Penderecki's opera, "the dynamic and tension-evoking sound of a tritone belongs, in accordance with tradition, to the world of Satan (cf. medieval *diabolus in musica*)" (Chłopicka 145).[14] Bound together—or, rather, split apart—by the tritone, Adam and Eve produce the sound of Satanic evil.

Matters get worse, not better. Adam's and Eve's vocal lines gradually converge, but instead of merging in a perfect unison, they get stuck on another profoundly dissonant interval: A♭–A♮ (see Example 4.1.2.1). After a tense moment during which Eve rapidly repeats her A♮ as she sings "happened to thyself," while Adam sustains an A♭ as he sings "you," their vocal lines diverge again; but they cannot seem to avoid repeating the same dissonant interval. Eve reaches up to a C♯ and Adam soon thereafter drops to a C♮ (Example 4.1.2.2). A♭–A♮ and C–C♯: these chromatic intervals—that is an, an interval between a pitch and another pitch only a half-scale-degree distant from it—produce an expressively discordant sound, conveying the simmering tension between husband and wife. This interval represents a fundamental disagreement: Adam and Eve take up the same pitch identity, A, but one of them understands it as a natural pitch, and the other as an accidental. This tonal disagreement suggests a larger disagreement, a different way of seeing the same world. Penderecki is invoking a formal musicological term as a pun to express the relationship between Adam and Eve. A chromatic interval such as A♭–A♮ or C–C♯ is a *false relation*, when a pitch and its accidentally modified version are sounded simultaneously.[15] Adding to the characterization of the tritone, the composer presents another musical interval that stands as a metaphor for the relationship between Adam and Eve. Theirs is a *false relation*: a compromised, degraded version of the harmonious marriage they enjoyed before the Fall. This use of music as metaphor begins to reveal Penderecki's realization of Miltonic musical theory.

Fractured into a complicated discord of incompatible rhythmic, stylistic, and tonal worlds, Adam and Eve offer a strikingly expressive mimesis of quarreling. But Penderecki also encodes in these strained sounds of human discord a metaphorical representation of what it means to be fallen: Adam and Eve *cannot sing together*. In this simple but devastating musical metaphor, Penderecki equates the musical *topoi* of rhythmic, stylistic, and tonal disunity with metaphysical disunity. Not only marriage but holistic human experience, experience authorized and emboldened by God, has been ruptured by the Fall. What the opera images as the condition of fallenness is a music of rhythmic, stylistic, and tonal dislocation, the shattering of unity into competing vocalities.

Like Milton himself, as I argued in Chapter 2, Penderecki understands music as at once a sensuous acoustic phenomenon and a metaphor representing the human condition. Handel strove to solve the problem of cacophony, to imagine what it could sound like in tonal harmony. Penderecki has taken on a more subtle problem. What does *fallenness* sound like? To answer the question, Penderecki draws on the potential of music to signify both through its mimetic sounds and its potential for metaphor. Enfranchised by the vast range of textures and harmonies of post-tonal music, Penderecki sonorously evokes human fallenness as a condition of anguish, confusion, and divisiveness.[16] At the same time, Penderecki configures the vivid soundworld of his opera to stand as a metaphor for fallenness. The composer has found a way to realize Miltonic musical theory in practical musical sound.

In "At a Solemn Music," which I examined in Chapters 1 and 2, Milton understands the effect of the Fall as a *musical* disruption, a "harsh din" breaking the metaphorical "fair music" of obedience (Milton, "At a Solemn Music" ll. 18, 19). Penderecki realizes the metaphorical "harsh din" of fallenness not just as harmonic dissonance—itself a common feature of post-tonal music—but as rhythmic and stylistic dissonance, too. The opera is set in the key and time-signature of fallenness. If fallenness begets musical disunity, however, then one might well imagine the obverse, that musical unity implies the metaphysical wholeness of prelapsarian innocence—what Milton in "At a Solemn Music" calls the "state of good" (l. 24). For Penderecki in *Paradise Lost*, is such unified music—and the condition of innocence it would represent—forever unrecoverable? What would such music sound like?

Penderecki and Fry give a clue in another striking departure from their source. Milton's epic denouement sees Adam and Eve departing from Paradise:

> The world was all before them, where to choose
> Their place of rest, and providence their guide:
> They hand in hand with wandering steps and slow,
> Through Eden took their solitary way.
> (Milton, *Paradise Lost* 12.646–649)

The poet evokes a temperate blend of sadness and hope. To the sorrow of being banished forever from Paradise as punishment for their sin, Milton adds the radiant wonder of exploration, as Adam and Eve set out into an uncharted world. Still, while Providence may guide humanity, Adam and Eve must choose their place of rest themselves. The necessity of human choice is the moral imperative with which Milton closes his poem.

Penderecki and Fry have an altogether different vision in mind:

> The World is all before them,
> Where to choose
> Their place of rest,
> And Providence their guide.
> Through the world's wilderness
> Long wanders man,
> Until he shall hear and learn

> The secret power
> Of harmony, in whose image he was made.
> (Fry and Penderecki 22)

After quoting Milton's penultimate lines, Fry replaces Milton's close-up image of Adam and Eve with a larger historical perspective. This historical view yields the promise that humanity's journey through history will ultimately end with the restorative power of music. For now, however, that musical power remains "secret."[17]

Rather than leave it to the audience to discover that music after leaving the opera theater, Penderecki in fact embeds it in the opera itself. The composer constructs the unfolding musical action as a heroic effort to uncover the secret power of restorative harmony—to restore to the shattered music of disunity the primal unity that has, by the time the opera begins, already been lost. But where can such music of unity be found?

One might think immediately of the prelapsarian life of Adam and Eve. But even here, in the unfallen innocence of the first man and woman, Penderecki allows only a partial recovery of musical and metaphysical unity. In one of Fry and Penderecki's small but meaningful adjustments to Milton's plot, the operatic Satan arrives in Eden in time to witness the very first meeting of Adam and Eve. The archfiend beholds with anguish first the beauty of the first human beings, then, in a double torment, their ensuing marital union:

SATAN
My thoughts pursue with wonder.
I could love them.

EVE
How beauty is excelled
By manly grace
And wisdom, which
Alone is truly fair.

ADAM (*Addressing GOD*)
Fairest this of all thy gifts
I now see bone of my bone,
Flesh of my flesh — —

BOTH
One heart, one soul.

Music as Sound and Metaphor in Penderecki's Paradise Lost   101

COURTSHIP AND MARRIAGE OF ADAM AND EVE.
(*Dance*) [...]
(*ADAM and EVE consummate their marriage.*)
(Fry and Penderecki 10)

What should by rights be the crowning moment of unity in the prelapsarian world—the spiritual and physical union of Adam and Eve—emerges in queasy proximity to the fundamental agent of evil. Penderecki registers the proximity in his musical setting (see Example 4.2).

Example 4.2 Adam and Eve declare their marriage
(Penderecki p. 161, system 1, mm. 1–6)

© 1978 SCHOTT MUSIC, Mainz–Germany. Reproduced by permission. All rights reserved.

As Adam and Eve declare their marriage, they join together to sing the phrase "One heart, one soul" (Example 4.2.1.3–4). The libretto offers an explicit image of unity that encourages the composer to construct a music of unity that can shore up what has thus far been the shattered fallenness of the operatic soundworld. Penderecki partly obliges. Adam and Eve *do* sing in perfect rhythmic unison, and their stylistic mode, too, is unified—both sing in a gently expressive *pianissimo*. In tonal terms, their phrase begins well enough, with Adam on a B and Eve on C (Example 4.2.1.3); while they form a dissonant minor second interval, these are both pitches from the C-major scale, and indeed, the orchestra provides a C-major harmony that unifies not only Adam and Eve but their entire soundworld. But the unity is short-lived. As they sing the word "heart," Adam and Eve diverge to the mildly dissonant B♭ and C♯; they briefly resolve to a more consonant harmony on their next word, "one," but then disaster strikes. At the crucial moment, as they sing the word "soul," Adam lands on E♭ and Eve on E♮. We have returned to a *false relation*—the sound and metaphor of fundamental dissonance. The false relation, as we recognized in the opening scene of the opera, sonorously expresses a dissonant anguish even as it stands as a metaphor for metaphysical disunity. At the moment of marriage Adam and Eve come tantalizingly close to musical unity but ultimately end up in different tonal worlds. If is a shattering moment. The fallenness of the opera infiltrates even the most intense instant of prelapsarian innocence.

Why is prelapsarian marriage tainted by disunity? Satan's secret vantage of the marital rites would seem the readiest explanation. Recall the similar scene in Milton's poem, in which Satan gains his first glimpse of Adam and Eve as they first appear in the epic: "the fiend / Saw undelighted all delight, all kind / Of living creatures new to sight and strange: / Two of far nobler shape erect and tall [...] seemed lords of all" (Milton, *Paradise Lost* 4.285-289; 290). The reader's sight of Adam and Eve is mediated by Satan's voyeurism. Similarly, Penderecki's music registers Satan's perverse perspective but at an earlier stage of the first human relationship. But if it is merely the presence of Satan that inflects the musical representation of marriage, we can assume that the marriage itself is indeed unified. If the marriage is not in fact compromised by disunity, then it is our fallen experience as an audience that the operatic soundworld registers.

Penderecki and Fry deepen our consciousness of fallenness as an audience through the careful design of their plot. The marriage occurs, we recall, in flashback, that is, after, in the progression of the plot,

Music as Sound and Metaphor in Penderecki's Paradise Lost

Adam and Eve have already fallen. Their musical false relation at the moment of marriage recognizes that their relationship has already, in the audience's experience of unfolding events, fallen. As an audience, we hear the marital unity of the unfallen Adam and Eve through the veil of fallenness that is both the starting condition of the opera and our own condition in human time outside the diegetic world of the opera itself. The precious unity Adam and Eve so nearly achieve is irrevocably compromised.

Another moment of potential musical unity occurs late in the second act, after the action catches up to the present moment and repeats the human fall. But this postlapsarian moment of unity turns out to be even more profoundly compromised than the marriage of Adam and Eve: it is the unity of war. As Michael relates the course of future human history to Adam, war is glossed in a violent choral setting, "Concourse in arms" (see Example 4.3; recording: Act 2, part ii, 14:08ff).

CHORUS
Concourse in arms,
Fierce faces threatening war,
On each hand slaughter
And gigantic deeds!
    (Fry and Penderecki 20)

Example 4.3 "Concourse in arms"
(Penderecki p. 381, system 1, mm. 1–3, vocal parts)
© 1978 SCHOTT MUSIC, Mainz–Germany. Reproduced by permission. All rights reserved.

Strikingly, the chorus is asked to sing the opening phrase in precise rhythmic and tonal unison.[18] Set in coloratura—that is, rapid, technically difficult vocal passagework—this unison challenges a chorus with a moment of technical derring-do. The virtuosity serves a metaphorical purpose.

If unison is a metaphor representing unity, then Penderecki suggests that fallen humanity is unified only in a universal desire for war. In a fallen world, the opera suggests, the primary unifying impulse is to destroy one another. Penderecki plays, I think, on the etymology of the word *concourse*, which derives via Old French from the Latin *concursum*, "running together" (*OED,* "concourse, *n.*"). As Milton originally employs it in *Paradise Lost,* "concourse" refers simply to a "hostile encounter" or battle (*OED,* "concourse, *n.*1.b.").[19] But Penderecki seems to draw on the original etymology in two senses. First, he directs the chorus to "run together" in the sense that they perform "running" scales in unison. Second, the composer hears the ironic homonymic potential relating the enmity of Milton's *concourse* with its opposite, *concord,* and presents a moment in which the chorus is unified, in concord, in precise alignment against great odds—that is, the odds of maintaining unison while performing difficult rapid scales. The singers' virtuosity expresses the crazed collective bloodthirstiness of fallen humanity.

Penderecki advances his characterization of war by splintering the chorus into two competing halves, one of which begins to sing a four-part harmonization of *Dies irae,* the atmospheric ancient plainchant liturgical setting describing the apocalypse.[20] Meanwhile, the other half of the choir continues to sing "Concourse in arms," and the two settings become interwoven (see Example 4.4; recording: Act 2, part 2, 14:33 ff.). As it develops, the entire gigantic two-choir setting comes to be governed by the *cantus firmus* of the *Dies irae.* The composer achieves a striking effect in which the unification of vast separate forces sonorously evokes not a sense of abiding structure but rather a terrifying sense of chaotic disorder. At the same time, this complex musical structure operates as a metaphor to imply that the unifying impulse to wage war is a drive towards apocalyptic self-annihilation.[21]

Music as Sound and Metaphor in Penderecki's Paradise Lost   105

Example 4.4 Part of the chorus begins singing "*Dies irae*" as the rest of the chorus continues to sing "Concourse in arms"

(Penderecki pp. 383–384, vocal parts)

© 1978 SCHOTT MUSIC, Mainz–Germany. Reproduced by permission. All rights reserved.

The two choirs join together to sing the final words of the setting, "And gigantic deeds," in huge, unified homophonic chords (see Example 4.5). As the united super-chorus enunciates a climactic statement of war's carnage, Penderecki composes a moment of perfect unity—unity in destruction. This is not a restoration of primal prelapsarian unity but its ultimate dissolution. If this is the "secret power of harmony" that "man [...] shall hear and learn," it is the secret only of his own destruction (Fry and Penderecki 22).

One final instance of compromised musical unison achieves not a recovery of prelapsarian unity but instead the same destruction evoked by the "Concourse" chorus. This final example is the triumphant unison singing of Sin and Death as they observe Michael's prophetic vision of war (see Example 4.6):

Example 4.5 The chorus singing *Dies irae* and the chorus singing "Concourse in arms" unite to conclude the setting

(Penderecki pg. 387, mm. 1–3, vocal parts)

© 1978 SCHOTT MUSIC, Mainz–Germany. Reproduced by permission. All rights reserved.

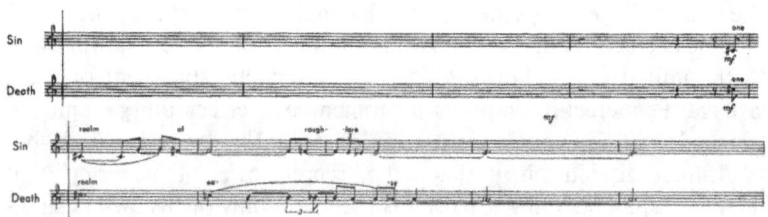

Example 4.6 Sin and Death sing "one realm" together

(Penderecki p. 390, Sin and Death's vocal parts)

© 1978 SCHOTT MUSIC, Mainz–Germany. Reproduced by permission. All rights reserved.

Music as Sound and Metaphor in Penderecki's Paradise Lost 107

Occurring shortly after the chorus finishes singing "Concourse in arms," Sin and Death's rhythmically and tonally unified utterance emerges as the symbolic source of that unison choral setting. Penderecki explicitly ties the two settings together: When Death sings "Ours now is all the world, / A world forfeit to Death!" (Fry and Penderecki 21), the composer sets the word "Ours" with the same downward-running chromatic scale motif on which the chorus sings "Concourse" (see Example 4.7):

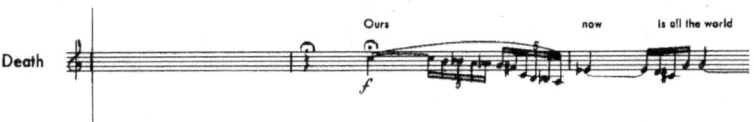

Example 4.7 Death sings the "concourse in arms" motif—see also Example 4.3.1.2
(Penderecki p. 389, system 1, mm. 1–3, Death's vocal part)
© 1978 SCHOTT MUSIC, Mainz–Germany. Reproduced by permission. All rights reserved.

This coloratura motif metaphorically represents the unifying bloodthirstiness of fallen humanity. *Ours,* indeed. As they slaughter their brethren in war, fallen humans become Death's possession. Sin and Death are not only the musical, but also the metaphoric source of the fallen human urge to slaughter one another.

Only the final defeat of Death and Sin, then, can cancel out their music of destructive unison, as well as the rhythmic dislocation, fractured tonality, and stylistic divisiveness engendered by fallenness. This, at last, is the key to the "secret power" of harmony. Only one act can defeat Death and Sin: the Son of God's decision to sacrifice himself to pay the debt of humanity's original sin. How Penderecki chooses to represent this act of self-sacrifice offers yet another major divergence from Milton's poem. In Milton's epic, the Son's sacrifice is strikingly proleptic—it occurs in Book 3, long before Adam and Eve fall in Book 9 or are put on trial in Book 10. But for Penderecki and Fry, the Son—whom the libretto labels "Messias," the Latin or German version of Messiah—volunteers to sacrifice himself immediately after Adam and Eve fall in the second act, as the opera catches up to its own beginning. After this second presentation of the fall occurs, God's Voice is heard: "Man disobeying, / He with his whole posterity must die" (Fry and Penderecki 17). Messias appears to plead on Man's behalf. In response, God exclaims, "No, He must die, / Unless some other / Willingly will pay / The death on his behalf. / Where shall we find such love?" (Fry and Penderecki 17). Messias responds:

108   *Milton in Music*

> Father, behold me, then,
> Me for him, life for life, I offer.
> (Fry and Penderecki 17)

This is the quiet climax of Penderecki's opera. The orchestra ceases to play. When music finally emerges into the reverent silence, it is not the orchestra but an unaccompanied chorus that we hear. Silence bleeds into sound, but the sound is different. Conditioned by the dissonant soundworld of the opera, the ear takes a moment to adjust. Then we hear it: the chorus is singing a four-part chorale in Baroque style. It is no pastiche, no skillful imitation of a past music. This is not the music of Penderecki at all. In response to Messias' supreme act of self-sacrifice—the act that will redeem humankind and defeat Sin and Death—Penderecki inserts into his opera of fallenness a Bach chorale (see Example 4.8):

Example 4.8 The chorus sings a Bach chorale

(Penderecki p. 310: system 2, mm. 1–5, vocal parts and select instrumental parts; p. 311: system 1, mm. 1–5, vocal parts)

© 1978 SCHOTT MUSIC, Mainz–Germany. Reproduced by permission. All rights reserved.

The chorale text is a poetic English translation of "O große Lieb," from Bach's *St. John Passion*:

> O wondrous love, whose depths no heart has sounded,
> That brought Thee here by Sin and grief surrounded,
> We live, the pleasures of this world enjoying.
> And Thou art dying.
>
> (Penderecki pp. 310–312)[22]

Why has Penderecki abandoned his own music at the climax of his opera? And why select a chorale—and an obscure chorale, at that, from the less famous of Bach's two surviving Passion settings? A chorale is an expression of musical and religious unity. For Bach, in his Passions as in his cantatas, the chorales are settings of extant Lutheran hymns intended to be sung by the church congregation who formed the audience for this religious music. Chorales are thus user-friendly: in four-part harmony for the voice parts of soprano, alto, tenor, and bass, chorales are relatively simple to sing. While the harmony, as always with Bach, can be progressive and experimental, all voices work together towards consonance; all dissonances are resolved. The chorale, moreover, is a *homophonic* genre. Voice parts do not move with contrapuntal complexity against one another, but instead align in rhythmic profile. No virtuosity disrupts the hymnal style: chorales are slow, stately, and serene. What a chorale offers, then, is a self-effacing communal music of praise, unified in both sound and theological purpose.[23] Penderecki's choice of the *St. John Passion* is telling. The more difficult and less cathartic of Bach's two surviving Passions is notable for complex chromatic harmony and a turbulent portrayal of the events leading up to the crucifixion. The communal serenity of the chorales, in this Passion, is hard won.

For Penderecki, this hard-won chorale is the ultimate expression of primal musical and spiritual unity. Having staked out a post-tonal compositional style of abrasive dissonance, Penderecki seems to have found in the tonal art of Bach a musical and spiritual ideal. That ideal is what the composer chooses to recognize the redemption of fallenness in *Paradise Lost*. The musical style of the opera—built on a stylistic, tonal, and rhythmic fracturing of unity—is shored up by the fervent unity of a Bach chorale.[24] Here, at last, is the "secret power of harmony": the power to unite the divisiveness of fallen humanity. It is a moving act of musical restoration that brings the opera to a musical and spiritual climax in a moment of compositional self-renunciation. Soon, Sin and Death will gloat as Michael's vision reveals the future of sinful posterity. But for an instant, as the Son promises to sacrifice his life to save humankind, the soundworld of the opera is touched by a unified and redemptive beauty.

For Penderecki as for Milton, the Son's decision to sacrifice himself is the central device by which the redemptive narrative of *Paradise Lost* is achieved.[25] Both epic and opera register the import of the Son's decision in the very fabric of their medium. In the epic, Milton balances the Son's act of love in Book 3 with the redemption of Adam and Eve in their trial in Book 10. The poet thus sets up a structural chiasmus, a parallel between corresponding books mirrored around the central axis of the epic. It is scarcely an exaggeration to claim that *Paradise Lost* hinges on the Son's compassion for fallen humanity. For Penderecki, the recognition is carried out through texture rather than structure, but it is no less far-reaching. Messias's act of love knits up the dislocated and fractured soundworld of the opera into the sonority of redemptive unity. The opening fall of Adam and Eve fractures and dislocates musical unison; Messias's decision to sacrifice himself reverses that dislocation and restores—however briefly—true unison.

While the moment of transcendent unity is climactic, the opera is in some sense more impressive and telling—if not more moving—in the representation of pervasive fallenness that gives unity such meaning. For in his evocation of fallenness, Penderecki has forged music that operates both as a sonorous acoustic phenomenon and intricately signifying metaphor. The twentieth-century iconoclast has at last made good on Milton's fierce and demanding conviction that music both *sounds* and *means*. To be sure, Milton would have found Penderecki's dissonant musical idiom alien if not repugnant. Nonetheless, more than any other Milton adaptation I know, Penderecki achieves in real musical sound the poet's lofty theoretical ideals. Visionary in his own time and for centuries past it, Milton's theory of music is finally vindicated in the practical achievement of Penderecki's uncompromising opera.

Notes

1 I am grateful to David Ainsworth for his comments, in reviewing my manuscript for the press, regarding Penderecki's opera as more "pessimistic about humanity" than Milton's poem, which is itself, in Ainsworth's witty formulation, not "especially cheery." While I accept Ainsworth's sense of the opera's darker vision—I understand it as combining the bleak affect of *Samson Agonistes* with the plot of *Paradise Lost*—I hold, rather, that Milton is in *Paradise Lost* remarkably optimistic about human nature and human history.

2 Penderecki's libretto was written by the dramatist Christopher Fry (1907–2005). Penderecki himself had a crucial hand in fashioning the libretto—"I imposed my own vision of the work," the composer declared—but, given the difficulties of Milton's idiom, he entrusted writing the libretto to a respected English dramatist (quoted in Draus 173). When discussing matters of linguistic style in the libretto, I refer to Fry, but when appropriate, i.e., when discussing thematic and structural elements, I refer to Penderecki alone. For citations, I use "Fry and Penderecki," but in the Works Cited and Consulted, Fry is listed as the primary author of the libretto.

3 Fry and Penderecki's central emphasis on fallenness participates in what John Leonard describes as a general trend of Milton scholarship in the twentieth century: "Modern critics agree that the Fall of Adam and Eve is the climax of *Paradise Lost* and that book nine is the greatest of the poem's twelve books. This was not always the consensus" (Leonard 601). In this way, Fry and Penderecki's operatic rendering converges with the critical reception history of the poem. See Leonard, *Faithful Labourers: A Reception History of* Paradise Lost *(1667–1970)* (Oxford: Oxford UP, 2013).

4 As Penderecki and Fry do not provide scene divisions, I use the term *event* rather than *scene*. The plot sequence in Table 4.1 is my own representation of the operatic plot; the numbers I provide are for ease of reference rather than an attempt to divide the opera into scenes. For an alternative plot sequence, see Table 1 in Agnieszka Draus, "Krzysztof Penderecki, *Paradise Lost*. From Milton's Poem to the *sacra rappresentazione* Libretto," in *Krzysztof Penderecki's Music in the Context of 20th-Century Theater*, edited by Teresa Malecka (Kraków: Akademia Muzyczna, 1999), 175–176. Draus divides the action into scenes.

5 Fry and Penderecki diverge from Milton by referring to the Son of God as "Messias," a post-Classical Latin form of *messiah* used in Old English, the Renaissance, and as late as the twentieth century (*OED*, "Messiah, *n.*").

6 See Regina Chłopicka, "*Paradise Lost*: A Contemporary Interpretation of the Biblical Story of Salvation"; and especially Ray Robinson, "Some Problems of Instrumentation in Penderecki's Opera *Paradise Lost* (1975–78)" and Ewa Wójtowicz, "Some Harmonic Aspects of Krzysztof Penderecki's *Paradise Lost*," all in *Krzysztof Penderecki's Music in the Context of 20th-Century Theater*, edited by Teresa Malecka (Kraków: Akademia Muzyczna, 1999), 141–148, 149–160, 161–171. All refer to either the three separate "realms" or "worlds" of God, Satan, and humanity. Agnieszka Draus does note that the opera occurs "virtually in two locations only: in the Abyss of Hell and in the Garden of Paradise. There are no scenes in Heaven" (Draus 174). (This is not quite right, as in Act II, the libretto once specifies Heaven as a location [Libretto p. 18].) But Draus also argues that both Milton and Penderecki concern themselves with "the successive contrasting of scenes associated with the respective universes of God, Man, and Satan" (176). I want to argue that the "universe" of God—even by association—is precisely what the opera takes pains to omit.

7   Draus and Chłopicka have noted that the opera is concerned primarily with the world of man (Draus 174 and Chłopicka 143), but I argue instead that the opera is concerned with the narrative of fallenness and with confining itself to the spatial realms appropriate to fallenness: Hell and Earth.
8   Many eighteenth–and nineteenth-century opera composers evoke tension or disagreement between two or more singers, but the overwhelming expectation is that singers who sing at the same time will produce a harmonious ensemble. The opening scene of Mozart's *Don Giovanni* provides an emblematic example. Donna Anna denounces Don Giovanni as Leporello talks to himself in the background. Mozart achieves an electric tension not through dissonance or rhythmic asynchronicity, but rather by an ingenious intertwining of the vocal lines of Anna, Giovanni, and Leporello.
9   For subsequent references to measures within my musical examples, I use the following system: Example [# of Chapter]. [# of Example].[# of system].[# of measure]. Thus, Example 1, system 1, measure 1 would be written as Example 4.1.1.1. The timings provided refer to what seems to be the only available full recording of *Paradise Lost*, a performance posted on youtube.com, listed as a recording of the world premiere by the Lyric Opera of Chicago (Nov. 29, 1978). I provide timings cued to this recording, which is split into four arbitrarily divided parts: Act 1, part 1; Act 1, part 2; Act 2, part 1; and Act 2, part 2. For ease of reference, I cite timings within these four parts. In order to listen to the desired recording segment, enter "Penderecki Paradise Lost Act 1 part 1," "…Act 2 part 2," etc., into the youtube.com search tool. Full URLs for each segment are listed in the Works Cited and Consulted.
10 Regina Chłopicka notes that Penderecki employs various styles to create the "musical world of man," including "intonational *recitativo*" (Chłopicka 146). Chłopicka notes the use of *stile concitato* in the opera, but argues that this style is primarily associated with Satan and his cadre of fallen angels (146). If Chłopicka is correct, then it is suggestive that Adam's initial response to Eve is characterized by a Satanic mode of singing.
11 See, for example, the first chorus from Bach's cantata *Weinen, Klagen, Sorgen, Sagen* (BWV 12).
12 The libretto reads "harkened," but in one of several instances of disagreement, the musical score reads "harked" (Libretto: p. 1; Score: Act 1, m. 98).
13 The tritone is technically an augmented fourth, which in modern tuning, is enharmonic with—i.e., identical in pitch-content to—the diminished fifth. I would argue that we should understand the interval between Adam and Eve as a tritone for two reasons. First, as it is sung, the audience hears it as a tritone; second, more subtly, while Eve's is the higher of the two pitches, she sings first, and Adam subsequently adds his pitch to hers. In terms of sequence, Eve offers the "ground" pitch, $G_\flat$, and we can construe Adam's pitch, C, as existing "above" Eve's ground. If $G_\flat$ is the ground and C exists above it, then we have an augmented fourth.
14 Scott Murphy takes issue with Chłopicka's assertion: "Chłopicka claims that the opera associates the tritone with Satan […]. But the preponderance

of tritones in the melodic fabric of the opera generally dilutes the *diabolus* association [...]. [M]ore precisely, the tritone does not appear in Satan's vocal lines more often than those of any other character" (Murphy 239). Without scanting Murphy's analysis of the melodic and tonal construction of the opera, I think both Murphy and Chłopicka are correct: The *sound* of the tritone is strongly associated with Satan, even while the tritone figures heavily in what Murphy calls the "melodic fabric" of the entire opera. What this means, I think, is that the opera encodes the evil of fallenness, which is most strongly associated with Satan, in the building blocks of its harmony.

15 E.g., $G_\natural$ and $G_\sharp$, or $D_\natural$ and $D_\flat$. The term *false relation* is associated primarily with Renaissance vocal music—the period and genre to which Penderecki is referring with his opera's subtitle, *Sacra Rappresentazione*. This subtitle refers to a species of musical drama that predates the opera, somewhat resembling an oratorio or opera but not quite either. See, for example, Emilio de Cavalieri's *Rappresentatione di Anima & di Corpo* (1600). The critics who noticed the subtitle, such as Andrew Porter in *The New Yorker* (December 18, 1978 [Vol. 54]), 98, and Linda Marie Delloff in *Christian Century* (96.2 [January 17, 1979]), 53, were not quite convinced of the relevance of the label. Porter notes that Cavalieri's *Rappresentatione di Anima & di Corpo* "is the most famous example" of the genre (98).

16 Ray Robinson argues that in *Paradise Lost* (1975–78), Penderecki synthesizes a new style of modern orchestration that combines techniques from his own radically individual style in the 1950s and 1960s with more traditional devices inherited from the classical tradition, especially Wagner and late nineteenth-century music. See "Some Problems of Instrumentation in Penderecki's Opera *Paradise Lost* (1975–78)," in *Krzysztof Penderecki's Music in the Context of 20th-Century Theatre,* edited by Teresa Malecka (Kraków: Akademia Muzyczna, 1999), 149–160.

17 Critics such as Stanwood and Draus have noted these final lines as a departure from Milton (Stanwood paras. 8–9, Draus 178), but they miss the fact, pointed out by Andrew Porter in his 1978 *New Yorker* review, that the evocative phrase, "secret power of harmony," is in fact borrowed from *Paradise Regained* (Porter 98). There the phrase is used by Satan as he tempts Christ to indulge in Classical learning: "There [in Athens] thou shalt hear and learn the secret power / Of harmony in tones and numbers hit / By voice or hand" (*PR* 4.254–256). What for Milton was a Satanic temptation, Fry appropriates as a sign of providential grace. Following his librettist, Penderecki takes the phrase at face value, fashioning what Stanwood acutely calls a "triumphant" close to the opera (Stanwood para. 11), a brilliant D-major triad.

18 All four vocal parts sing a G, in the octave appropriate to their range, and then commence rapid identical passagework, maintaining their octave unison. (Sounding pitches at an octave is considered equivalent to unison.)

19 Milton's phrase, which Fry lifts and splits into two lines, comes from Book 11: "Concourse in arms, fierce faces threatening war" (Milton, *Paradise Lost* 11.641).

20 The ominous power of this chant has long made it a favorite of composers who wish to evoke death and destruction, from Berlioz, who uses it in the satanic final movement of his *Symphonie Fantastique*, to Liszt, who writes a set of variations on it for piano and orchestra entitled *Totentanz*, the "Dance of Death." Rachmaninov wove the theme into works from his first piano sonata to his *Rhapsody on a Theme of Paganini*.

21 Chłopicka notices Penderecki's use of the *Dies irae*, drawing attention to its technical musical purpose as a "*passacaglia* theme" (Chłopicka 147). But while Chłopicka understands the *Dies irae* allusion as contributing to the "apocalyptic vision of the future world" (147), she understands that vision as providing "a symbolic message of hope" (147). I concur that the last measures of the opera offer a radical vision of musical redemption— perhaps predicated, as I've suggested above, on Milton's own vision in "At a Solemn Music"—but I differ from Chłopicka in arguing that the use of the *Dies irae* is diametrically opposed to that vision.

22 These page numbers refer to the musical score, since the chorale text does not appear in the libretto. No translator seems to be cited in the musical score, but Andrew Porter identifies the translator as the Reverend J. Troutbeck, D.D. (Porter 90).

23 For a reappraisal of the art and performance practice of the chorales, see Robin A. Leaver, "Suggestions for Future Research into Bach and the Chorale: Aspects of Repertoire, Pedagogy, Theory, and Practice," in *Bach* 42.2 (2011), 40–63.

24 The chorale Penderecki selects, "O große Lieb," translated as "O wondrous love," nicely glosses the words of praise that the libretto, borrowing directly from Milton, subsequently gives to the chorus to describe Messias's act of sacrifice: "Love hath abounded" (Fry and Penderecki 17). Milton's God declares: "Love hath abounded more than glory abounds" (Milton, *Paradise Lost* 3.312).

25 Critics have failed to recognize the importance of the role Messias plays in the drama. Stanwood finds that "the Son appears abruptly, almost an afterthought, as 'Messias,' and then quite briefly near the end of Act 2" (Stanwood para. 9). Linda Marie Delloff blames Fry for reducing the role of Christ with respect to Milton: "Missing, too, from Fry's version is the important role played by Milton's Christ" (Delloff 53). See also Porter in the *New Yorker* (98).

Conclusion

This book has compared two richly challenging Miltonic texts—*Samson Agonistes* and *Paradise Lost*—to later musical adaptations of them by Handel and Penderecki. Beyond the intrinsic value of these comparisons, I hope to have shown the utility of juxtaposing literature with its musical counterparts. This method has the advantage of allowing us not only to grasp how music analyzes, through recreative interpretation, its literary sources, but also to inquire into the ways in which literature provokes musical adaptation in the first place. My approach can be illustrated concisely with a retrospective glance at one of Milton's earliest attempts to analyze music, in *L'Allegro* and its companion poem, *Il Penseroso*, set alongside a later musical adaptation of these poems by Handel: the delightful oratorio, *L'Allegro, il Penseroso ed il Moderato*. In *L'Allegro*, Milton has begun to think towards, but not yet fully developed, his mature model of music—consolidated in "At a Solemn Music," developed in *A Masque*, and scaled up to epic proportion in *Paradise Lost*—as simultaneously an acoustic phenomenon and a metaphor for the relationship of created beings to God.

Towards the close of *L'Allegro* Milton writes what is probably his most celebrated passage on music:

> And ever against eating cares,
> Lap me in soft Lydian airs,
> Married to immortal verse
> Such as the meeting soul may pierce
> In notes, with many a winding bout
> Of linked sweetness long drawn out,
> With wanton heed, and giddy cunning,
> The melting voice through mazes running;

> Untwisting all the chains that tie
> The hidden soul of harmony.
> (ll. 135–144)[1]

As the ebullient speaker modulates from the daytime "busy hum of men" (118) to the quieter charms of musical sound, the poem would seem to demonstrate the material, acoustic, and metaphorical qualities that distinguish the mature Milton's concept of music. But the resemblance is more superficial than actual. The dating of *L'Allegro* is not certain—in his Longman edition notes, Carey tentatively assigns it to summer 1631—but the treatment of music in the poem seems to me clearly to antedate the watershed treatment of music of "At a Solemn Music" (another uncertain dating; Carey thinks 1633). The model of music that emerges in *L'Allegro* anticipates the model staked out in "At a Solemn Music," but in *L'Allegro* it is not only incomplete but finally incoherent.

The nature of that incoherence is, however, elusive. The profound aesthetic pleasure of the passage, with its subtle variations in prosody and sinuous play of enjambments, tends to obscure the way in which Milton is—or is not—representing music itself. The passage ostensibly describes the actual sound of music, as the melodic contours of the "soft Lydian airs" are characterized by "many a winding bout / Of linked sweetness long drawn out." Milton seems to be describing both harmony and style: a Lydian air that is *melismatic*; that is, with multiple pitches sung without any break, *legato*, to a single syllable of text. But the concrete qualities of the musical imagery grow increasingly abstract. The closing couplet presents an allegory-in-miniature that makes the sound of music a pure abstraction as voice succeeds in "Untwisting all the chains that tie / The hidden soul of harmony." Why does Milton proceed from vivid musical images to allegorical abstraction?

It is illuminating to compare this passage with Handel's musical rendering of it in his fantastically inventive oratorio, *L'Allegro, il Penseroso ed il Moderato*. Working with two librettists, James Harris and Charles Jennens, Handel fashioned a debate between Mirth and Melancholy by splitting Milton's poems into brief sections and interleaving them. The resulting dialogue emerges as a series of airs (arias), accompanied recitatives, and airs with chorus. After two parts (rather than acts) treating the debate between Mirth and Melancholy, a new figure, Moderation—with new poetry by Jennens—enters in Part the Third to reconcile the two competing philosophies.[2] The passage on music from Milton's *L'Allegro*, "And ever against eating cares," is set as an air for treble or soprano, towards the close of Part the Second.³

The choice of key signature is immediately striking. Milton has invited a specific harmony—"Lydian airs"—but Handel instead writes an air in G minor. Why not write in the Lydian mode, or an imitation of it? As it turns out, that is not such a simple prospect. As John Carey points out, scholars have debated whether *Lydian* might refer either to the ancient Greek mode or to the medieval ecclesiastical mode (Carey, note to *L'Allegro* 1. 136).⁴ Handel could surely have alluded to the Church mode, even if he did not know the Greek one. Yet the composer conspicuously avoids any modal inflection of his melody, let alone a modal harmonic setting.⁵ In ignoring the invitation to the Lydian mode, Handel demonstrates, I think, that Milton's description is in fact deliberately indeterminate; Milton invokes a rhetorical *idea* of music rather than its actual sound.

Handel is also keenly responsive to the text when it comes to the melismatic quality Milton describes (see Example C.1):

Example C.1 "With many a winding bout": melisma on "many" (Handel p. 112, system 3)⁶

The composer unfolds a long mimetic melisma of nineteen notes that continually circles back on itself as it ascends in an embellished scale. What is slightly unexpected is *where* Handel places his melisma: on the first syllable of "many," rather than on the more obvious invitation to text-painting on the words "winding" or "bout." The subtle effect is to double the mimesis: Handel enacts both the "winding bout" of sound, the long circular arabesque of melody curling around itself, but also the *many*-ness of the singer's "notes," which proliferate on the very word that describes them. Both sensible and subtle, Handel's musical rendering here reminds the listener that Milton has imagined an actual musical sound in his poetry.

But as the air continues, the gap in Milton's text between the description of music and what music actually sounds like becomes increasingly apparent. As the passage turns from the concrete musical description of melisma towards the abstraction of allegory, Handel begins to ignore the specific poetic content, indeed to avoid mimetic effects altogether. With his closing allegory-in-miniature, Milton provides an intellectual and aesthetic climax. At the corresponding moment, Handel provides a musical anti-climax (See Example C.2):

Example C.2 Winding down the air
(Handel p. 113, system 3; p. 114, system 1)

Handel reduces the harmonic and melodic eventfulness of his setting, initially settling on an unchanging single reciting pitch, D, as the singer first sings "untwisting all the chains," and then methodically returning to the tonic, the home key of the aria. Milton's ecstatic allegorical vision of the essence of music—"The hidden soul of harmony"—is for Handel simply the basic fact of the aria's home key. The return to the tonic is scarcely a visionary revelation of the soul of harmony such as the poet imagined. But what is a composer to do with what is a deliberately hyperbolical poetic allegory? The soul of harmony is a clear idea for a *reader*, but it is not a precise image for a composer seeking mimetic imagery. Where in *Samson Agonistes* Handel was confronted with an acoustic phenomenon, cacophony, that he refused to try to represent mimetically, here the composer is faced with a textual evocation of sound that does not invite representation at all. As the *L'Allegro* air progresses, Handel's music itself grows increasingly abstracted from the text it is setting, until finally it turns to the ratification of its own musical harmonic architecture in lieu of a mimetic response to the text.

What Handel's air finally reveals about Milton's thinking about music in *L'Allegro* is that in this early poem, music is not imagined as both sound and metaphor. It is imagined purely as sound. In the later "At a Solemn Music," Milton would present music as both an acoustic object and as an expression of metaphorical relation to God. Earlier, in *L'Allegro*, the poet deploys metaphor only as a poetic device to evoke the sensuous aesthetic qualities of music. This is a key distinction. Music is not *itself* a metaphor; poetry *uses* metaphor to evoke music. The paradox is that the resulting representation of music is in fact, by Milton's later standards, remarkably—and I would argue deliberately—vague. Rather than deploying poetic language as a vehicle for the clear exposition of a precise model of music, Milton evokes the aesthetic effects of music with poetic language that, even as it becomes more abstract as an evocation of musical sound, also becomes progressively more interesting than the music it is describing. As the account of the musical melody proceeds, that is, it grows ever less concrete in terms of the actual sonic content of music, and ever more brilliant as poetry. The intellectual complexity of allegory—rather than any vividly precise model or sound-image of music—brings the passage to its aesthetic climax. The larger effect is to substitute the literary means of poetry for the vivid description of music, to point the reader's attention increasingly away from the actual sound of music towards a poetic simulation of how such music makes the listener feel. Yet the text explicitly claims it is describing the actual sound of music.

This is what I mean by Milton's incoherence. Metaphor and allegory are here inconsistently deployed, at first to describe musical sound but increasingly to point towards the literariness of poetry itself; music itself is never represented as both sound and metaphor. This passage is the work of a sophisticated young poet who has not yet worked out the importance of music in his own thought. Just a few years before writing "At a Solemn Music," Milton's account of music in *L'Allegro* is a poetic tour de force but almost wholly lacking in the aesthetic and moral distinctiveness that makes the later poem a watershed moment in the poet's career. The reason, I think, lies in theology: *L'Allegro* is not a religious poem. In a secular setting, without the religious subject matter of "At a Solemn Music," Milton lacks both a theological rationale and a theological apparatus to ratify music as the ultimate Christian art.[7]

This pairing of an early Miltonic representation of music and Handel's musical rendering of it offers a case study in the method of my book as a whole, and how I hope it can be expanded to mount further work on both Milton and other poets. First, I invite literary scholars to attend more closely to how poetry imagines music and, more broadly, sound—in particular for the poets who cherish music, among them Shakespeare, Milton, Dryden, and Herbert in the early modern period, or, say, Dickinson, Yeats, Langston Hughes, and Terrance Hayes in later eras. For his part, Milton comes to conceive music as a material phenomenon that is both sound and metaphor, a fusion of two separate aesthetic dimensions. The rationale for the fusion is theological, as a means of praising the Christian God and revealing the ontology of his created universe. But another poet might easily conceive music as sound and metaphor in a secular context. Since writing poetry about music forces the poet to explore the relation between non-semantic musical sound and semantic meaning—even when read aloud as sound, poetry must commit to some semantic meaning, while wordless music has no inherent semantic content—any poet writing about music must decide whether music will emerge on its own terms, as sound without semantics, or as a vehicle for conveying meaning, a metaphor or symbol or allegory. To read poetry about music aloud is to be reminded that poetry is *not* music; but some poets urge their medium towards musical qualities, while some—like the mature Milton—use their medium to posit an aesthetic complexity in music as both sound and metaphor. Still others—like the younger Milton in *L'Allegro*—settle for a mimesis of the listener's receptive attitude toward music. What is essential for the critic, I would argue, is always to pay attention to what poets say about music in their poetry, to attend to how such poetry sounds as well as how it means, since it provides a referendum on how the poet conceives the relation between sound and sense. We must listen to such poetry, to its prosody and sonic strategies for organizing meaning, and let our ear be our "best guide" (*A Masque* l. 170) to its marshaling of poetic strategies.

Second, I invite literary scholars to listen to musical adaptations of poets they study. By attending to Handel's setting of Milton's *L'Allegro*, we grasped the extent to which Milton's setting prefers poetic virtuosity to actual engagement with musical sound. We also grasped the thinness of Milton's imagination of music at this early stage of his career, despite the intellectual and prosodic brilliance of his verse. The resulting challenge for Handel is not one of finding a way to represent an unrepresentable sound, as it is with cacophony in *Samson Agonistes*, but instead one of not being given any precise account of sound to render in the first place.

By attending to musical adaptations of poets, and in particular adaptations of poets who are themselves musical, literary critics can avail themselves of a mode of interpretation that has been mostly of interest to the words-and-music specialist. Even without the expertise of the professional musicologist, the literary critic can gain access to new analytical dimensions that can enhance our interpretive work. We can observe how composers use mimetic effects in music to render the poetic text, and then work that understanding into a new reading of the original poetic effects; we can discern how musical rhythms either preserve or disrupt the prosody and lineation of a poetic text, allowing that understanding to enhance our scansion of the original poetry; we can explore how composers or librettists emend or revise local and global textual features, revitalizing our understanding of the construction of the original text; we can investigate how music preserves or alters the genre of the literary source text, thus helping to reveal the original textual genre.

On this last count, of textual genre, Handel is of great help when it comes to textual genre. What precisely is the genre of Milton's *L'Allegro*? Is it a philosophical poem? A poem about youth and maturation? A poem of aesthetics? Handel's innovative oratorio splits Milton's *L'Allegro* into coherent lyric fragments and interweaves them with coherent fragments of *Il Penseroso*. The composer reveals to us something about how Milton achieves the unusual form of *L'Allegro* (and *Il Penseroso*). He weds together a broad range of separate speech acts and lyric genres that themselves govern articulable subsections of the poetic whole—command, story-telling, aubade, pastoral, serenade, and so forth. Yeats says in "Adam's Curse" that to produce poetry is "to articulate sweet sounds together" (l. 10).[8] Milton's art in *L'Allegro* and *Il Penseroso* is to articulate small blocks of lyric together to create a larger lyric. The genre of each poem is a compound of multiple smaller genres, an encyclopedic technique of concatenation and assimilation. It is a technique Milton will develop further, and master, in his greatest lyric poem, *Lycidas*. Listening to Handel's oratorio, and observing his rather strange musical form, points towards the distinctive strategy of Milton's original form and genre.

Just as in this brief case study of Milton's and Handel's renderings of *L'Allegro*, this book unites the two halves of the puzzle—"Milton on Music" and "Milton in Music"—to form a suggestive picture. Beyond illustrating the nature of my approach in the book and suggesting the future possibilities in this field for Milton scholars and scholars of lyric and epic poetry, this case study should also suggest how musicologists might profit from literary analysis. In the study of text-based, text-inspired, or non-textual narrative music, the musicologist can draw on poetry as a lens to study music.

The case study of Milton and Handel also points to the larger stakes of my argument in this book. Superficial as it might be in comparison with his later accounts of music, the representation of music in *L'Allegro* registers an enduring aspect of Milton's engagement with music: passionate sensory response. One of the most cerebral poets of the early modern period, Milton might easily have found music a purely intellectual vehicle, all sense and no sensibility. Yet music was for Milton never simply a metaphor. From his earliest years, it was a constant presence in his world. Drawing on what was evidently a personal experience of inspiring aesthetic delight, he accorded music a crucial role in his poetry. It is difficult to grasp Milton's global achievement as a poet without coming to terms with his poetry on music. In repeatedly deploying his acoustic–metaphoric model for music after developing it in "At a Solemn Music," Milton remained remarkably consistent, allowing us to track how the poet unified his aesthetic and theological ideas over decades of diverse poetic compositions. But at the same time, Milton's representation of music—so carefully premeditated as it was—also galvanized an unplanned intellectual evolution, a progression towards the monist materialism that, in its full expression in *Paradise Lost*, makes the universe of his God one of the strangest and most thrilling visions—and soundscapes—in Western literature. Finally, in Milton's poetic treatment of music, we see revealed, if never fully reconciled, the competing qualities of conservatism and radicalism—aesthetic, theological, and political—that define Milton and continue to make him a figure at once canonical and divisive. I hope that we will think further about Milton's thinking about music, for to consider Milton's poetry on music is to occupy, perhaps more intensely than in any other domain of the poet's work, the tense contradictions of Milton's art and thought.

Superseding the cautious, partial materialism of thinkers such as Thomas Wright, Milton increasingly conceived music as a radically materialist phenomenon that in turn affected and revealed the materiality of the human soul. Yet Milton's use of music was, or tried to be, conservative, in service of the Christian God whose ways he intended in his poetry to "justify" (*Paradise Lost* 1.26). The tension between radicalism and conservatism proved productive rather than crippling. Milton tried to control music in his poetry, tried to harness it to pursue his most ardently cherished ends. Even as he succeeded, music transformed his mind.

For those fit though few composers who have tried to give to Milton's daunting works a musical afterlife, something of his questing, restive, contradictory spirit finds its way into their works. Handel's delightful *L'Allegro* air makes the most of a young Milton's not fully coherent representation of music, but in the very different challenge posed by *Samson Agonistes*, Handel encountered Milton's invitation to render cacophony in art with evasive ingenuity. *Samson* is a magnificently entertaining oratorio. But by avoiding the aesthetic problem of cacophonous noise, Handel contradicts both the letter of Miltonic music theory and the spirit of Miltonic formal innovation. On the one hand, Handel implies music incapable of functioning as both sound and metaphor at once. On the other hand, with its refusal to confront or render mimetically the aesthetic breakage of cacophony, Handel's musical adaptation of *Samson* is a deliberate rejection of Milton's formal experimentalism. Handel's treatment of cacophony would seem to position the composer within the aesthetically conservative spectrum of responses to Milton in the long eighteenth century. Poets and thinkers from Peter Hume to Addison to Cowper to Pope to Dr. Johnson[9] showed a remarkable acuity in observing Milton's poetics but remained also uneasy with the more radical dimensions of Milton's epic achievement. In aesthetic reception, we might take as characteristic Pope's reduction of Miltonic epic into the social satire of *The Rape of the Lock*. The musical reception of Milton, at least as far as Handel goes, approximates Milton's scale in *Samson Agonistes* but offers a similarly subtle mixture of respect and revision, transformation and appropriation, fitting Milton into the values of eighteenth-century aesthetic order.

In political terms, however, Handel's work is less straightforward. Handel's musical rendering of the Philistines sharply divides him from his literary Miltonic source. Where Milton restricts the Philistines to a series of individual antagonists, Handel gives them a chorus of their own, representing them as a resounding community of people. Moreover, as Ellen Harris has argued, Handel does not flinch from representing the death cries of the Philistines with pathos and dignity:

> Handel's settings [...] display a deep sympathy for all victims, at the very least in the portrayal of their suffering [...]. When Samson brings down the temple of Dagon on himself and his foes, the crushing of the Philistines is set by Handel in a harrowing chorus.
>
> (Harris 298)

Milton draws on the Philistines' shrieks as a vehicle for his experimental representation of cacophony; Handel allows the Philistines to sing their own funerary music. In so doing, the composer accords the Philistines a tragic dignity Milton's tragedy deliberately withholds. Milton's famous tolerance for freedom of expression, articulated most powerfully in *Areopagitica*, does not extend to tolerance for pagan religion in the Old Testament.

Handel's more aesthetically conservative art is in this respect politically more progressive than Milton's fierce justification of Samson as champion of his people. In its fashioning of two equally represented national communities, Handel's *Samson* espouses something like a liberal tolerance for the *fact* of pagan society in the Old Testament, if not for the cultural values of such societies. Milton's *Samson Agonistes* instead celebrates the destruction of pagan society. While the sense of Milton as justifying Samson's genocidal actions is not new—John Carey reignited a longstanding controversy with his inflammatory 2002 piece, "A Work in Praise of Terrorism? September 11 and *Samson Agonistes*"—I would add that Milton's formal experimentation actually rises to a peak as he shows strongest support for the violence of the Old Testament God.[10] It is through Milton's treatment of sound as a sensuous material phenomenon encoding moral meaning—here, the offstage cacophony Samson unleashes expresses the ethical cacophony of the tragedy—that a portrait of the artist as espousing radical aestheticism and cultural conservatism comes into sharpest focus.

Writing in the aftermath of World War II, Krzysztof Penderecki came to *Paradise Lost* with a blend of formal experimentalism and theological, if not cultural, conservatism that in some ways echoes Milton's own. Penderecki never, so far as I know, composed an adaptation of *Samson Agonistes*, but my intuition is that his vision of *Paradise Lost* is indebted to the blighted world of Milton's late tragedy. Where Milton designs *Paradise Lost* to affirm God's providential care for humanity despite the "tragic notes" of the human fall (*Paradise Lost* 9.5–6), Penderecki composes an opera that is almost everywhere shot through with the dissonant sounds of fallenness. Even before they fall, Adam and Eve seem, like Milton's Samson, to be in "total eclipse" (Milton, *Samson Agonistes* 1. 81). In ways that exceed Milton's own perspective of fallen readerly experience—fallen humans are capable of reform, Milton holds, and as Stanley Fish has famously argued, the poem is designed to help us along[11]—Penderecki never allows the opera's listener to forget that we, too, are hopelessly fallen, that everything we hear is compromised, dissonant. Yet it is in the very service of this more pessimistic account of human experience that Penderecki unfolds a brilliantly inventive formal aesthetics.[12] In music that is at once acoustically expressive and metaphorically charged, Penderecki succeeds in realizing Milton's theory of music as acoustic object and metaphor. The resulting score combines a bleak vision of human experience with a visionary musical aesthetics. Milton's own concept of music takes on real form, itself affirmed as both visionary and, ultimately, realizable.

Penderecki's musical response to Milton reveals, by sharp contrast, the poet's own fundamental optimism about God's providence and human experience, even as it enacts the poet's ideals for how music should operate in the fallen human world.[13] If the world is fallen, music should still sound beautiful and hold ethical meaning, Milton argues. Penderecki concurs. Yet if, like Milton, Penderecki blends aesthetic innovation with the conservative goal of justifying God's providential ways to men, Penderecki also adopts as the climax of his opera an aesthetic conservatism that stands at odds with Milton's art.

As we have seen, Penderecki achieves a climactic recovery of prelapsarian unity only through a return to the music of Johann Sebastian Bach. This poignant act of repair, restoring the fractured quality of Penderecki's operatic soundworld, is also a humble surrender to the music of another composer, the most famous of Western and Christian composers. While Milton is far-reaching in his allusive plundering of prior art, he is fundamentally opposed to admitting the superiority of that art: at stake is the necessary superiority of the Christian God.[14] In Penderecki's self-abnegating recourse to Bach, however, the composer "turns off" his own music and allows Bach center stage. Penderecki finds the solution to human fallenness—the salvific "secret power / Of harmony" (Fry and Penderecki 22)—in the art of another, superior composer, a composer of the past. For Penderecki in *Paradise Lost*, music in a fallen world cannot help but register our fallenness; only a turn to the musical past can sound and be redemptive.

But music, for Milton, is not a thing of the past. Music is instead Janus-faced, pointing both back to the prelapsarian past, when we "with undiscording voice" sang in praise of God, but also looking into the redeemed future, when we will join God in heaven and once again "sing in endless morn of light" (Milton, "At a Solemn Music" ll. 17, 27). Looking backward and forwards in time, music also occupies the human plane in the present, even if it is at best in only a partially redeemed form like the Lady's song in *A Masque*. Even bad music, in the present, serves a purpose, helping us discern the complex moral ills that can be hidden in fair aesthetic forms. Like the Lady, if our "ear be true" (*A Masque* l. 169), we can recall the music of the prelapsarian past, think ahead to the music of the paradisal future, and live in the present with the moral and aesthetic satisfaction of listening discerningly to good music.

Penderecki may have realized one version of Milton's theory of music, but other, less pessimistic, versions have yet to be discovered. To take on Milton's thinking about music and attempt to render it into real music is no easy feat, as the complicated products of Handel's and Penderecki's musical imaginations testify. Yet to make the attempt is to be provoked into innovation, whether it be aesthetic, as with Penderecki, or political, as with Handel. Past musical adaptations of Milton have yet to be exhausted as sites of critical reception and innovative interdisciplinary response to a seminal poet; but I hope there will be future musical adaptations of Milton that approach even more closely than Penderecki to Milton's visionary theory of music as moral matter. Often taken as the poet of what Gordon Teskey calls "the origin," the poet who went back to the Christian beginning of things to try to explain how and why we are the way we are,[15] John Milton is also the poet of the future, at least if we try to think about and listen to music in the ways he advised, and perhaps try to create new music of the kind he uniquely imagined.

Notes

1 Quotations from Milton's shorter poetry are from the Longman 2nd edition of *The Complete Shorter Poems*, edited by John Carey.
2 For an account of the development of the libretto for *L'Allegro, il Penseroso ed il Moderato*, see Ruth Smith, "Milton Modulated for Handel's Music," in *Milton in the Long Restoration*, edited by Blair Hoxby and Anne Baynes Coiro (Oxford, UK: Oxford UP, 2016), 159–177, especially pp. 160–168, and "'Something of a Gayer Turn': Why Handel Laid Aside *Messiah* in 1740," Smith's liner notes essay for the Signum recording of *L'Allegro, il Penseroso ed il Moderato* (Signum Records, 2015). As Smith observes, Handel himself originally chose "At a Solemn Music" to serve as the text for the third part of his oratorio, but Jennens "recognised that Milton's ecstatic depiction of

a Christian heaven would subvert the integrity of the planned composition" (Smith, "'Something of a Gayer Turn'"). In other words, Jennens realized that *L'Allegro* and *Il Penseroso* are secular works, "At a Solemn Music" religious, and guided Handel towards a secular alternative.
3 The libretto alters Milton only in one line: where Milton has "Married to immortal verse" (l. 137), Jennens adjusts the text to "**Sooth me with** immortal verse" (Jennens and Harris, "And ever against eating cares" l. 3, emphasis added). I can only suppose that Jennens wished to clarify Milton's circuitous syntax by adjusting the past participial adjective to an imperative verb; or perhaps the composer preferred the long *o* vowel of "sooth" as a more euphoniously singable alternative to the short *a* of "Married."
4 The Greek mode might seem the more logical reading, since Plato rejects it in *Republic* 3.398–399 as conducive to indolence, and indolence is precisely what the mirthful speaker here desires; yet as far as actual musical sound goes, Milton would have been more likely to know the Church mode—and with its positive association with restorative energy, the Church mode is more a match for the speaker's temperament (Carey, note to *L'Allegro* l. 136).
5 G minor is far from any version of the Lydian mode, ancient Greek or medieval; in the more familiar medieval Church mode, the Lydian mode is equivalent to a modern diatonic F major scale with its fourth degree raised a half-tone to B natural.
6 All musical examples are drawn from the edition edited by Friedrich Chrysander, which is in the public domain and available online at imslp.org: https://s9.imslp.org/files/imglnks/usimg/0/00/IMSLP18743-PMLP03541-HG_Band_6.pdf.
7 In the corresponding passage on music in *Il Penseroso*, Milton does introduce a generically religious context as a setting for music, "the studious cloister" (l. 156), but it is in fact a secular account of a monastery as an exotic locale rather than a poem of genuine theological purpose. The passage on music in *Il Penseroso*, moreover, fails to rise to the rhapsodic heights of *L'Allegro*. In *Il Penseroso*, Milton splits the consolidated account of music from *L'Allegro* into two rather less poetically brilliant shorter sections: "And as I wake, sweet music breathe / Above, about, or underneath, / Sent by some spirit to mortals good, / Or the unseen genius of the wood" (151–154); "There let the pealing organ blow, / To the full-voiced choir below, / In service high, and anthems clear, / As may with sweetness, through mine ear, / Dissolve me into ecstasies, / And bring all heaven before mine eyes" (161–166). What is common to the account of music in *L'Allegro* and *Il Penseroso* is the quality of sweetness that Milton ascribes to musical sound, and a certain cautious materialism. In the first short passage in *Il Penseroso*, music shows the capacity to "breathe," as it does in *A Masque* (cf. ll. 554–555), and Milton gives it spatial location: "Above, about, or underneath." Later in the poem, the spatial presence of music comes into contact with the body: the "pealing organ" combines with "the full-voiced choir" to project "sweetness, through mine ear." But, crucially, the material soul

does not come into view. Instead, once music comes into the ear, the mode switches to the visual, as a vision of God's heaven is simulated "before mine eyes." Where *L'Allegro* specifies a mode of music, Lydian, *Il Penseroso* specifies musical forces and a genre, the anthem; but neither poem is interested, finally, in a consolidated model of music, and *Il Penseroso* is, however lovely in its melancholic account of transportive ecstasy, less virtuosic as poetry than *L'Allegro*.

8 See *The Collected Poems of W.B. Yeats*, edited by Richard J. Finneran, revised 2nd ed. (New York: Scribner, 1996), 80–81. I am grateful to Helen Vendler for reminding me of Yeats' succinct account of poetic craft.

9 For the recent identification of the first annotator of *Paradise Lost* as Peter Hume, rather than Patrick Hume, see David A. Harper, "The First Annotator of *Paradise Lost* and the Makings of English Literary Criticism," *SEL 1500–1900* 59.3 (Summer 2019), 507–530.

10 In 2002, John Carey ignited controversy with an article in *TLS*, "A Work in Praise of Terrorism? September 11 and *Samson Agonistes*," suggesting that Milton's Samson is a terrorist (6 September 2002), 15–16. The ensuing debate, heated as it was, sometimes yielded fresh insights into Milton's most interpretively challenging work. Among the notable responses: Stanley Fish, "'There is Nothing He Cannot Ask': Milton, Liberalism, and Terrorism"; David Loewenstein, "*Samson Agonistes* and the Culture of Religious Terror"; and Feisal G. Mohamed, "Confronting Religious Violence: Milton's *Samson Agonistes*." For a nuanced piece that essentially concurs with Carey, see Tobias Gregory, "The Political Messages of *Samson Agonistes*," *SEL 1500–1900* 50.1 (Winter 2010), 175–203.

11 *Surprised by Sin: The Reader in* Paradise Lost is Fish's seminal "reader response" account of Milton's epic. The reader is taught by Milton's epic, Fish argues, to be a better Christian (Berkeley and Los Angeles: U California P, 1971).

12 I am grateful to David Ainsworth, in his review of my book manuscript, for his suggestion, in line with my analysis in chapter 4, that Penderecki's opera is more "pessimistic about humanity" than Milton's poem.

13 In his review of my manuscript, David Ainsworth also declared that Milton's poem, too, is fairly pessimistic about human experience, if less so than Penderecki's opera; but I argue, to the contrary, that despite its partially "tragic" subject material (Milton, *Paradise Lost* 9.6), Milton's epic is essentially optimistic, indeed remarkably so, about God's providential plan for humanity. I am grateful to Ainsworth for helping me clarify, by contrast with his own reading, my sense of Milton's fundamental optimism.

14 For an account of Milton's technique of Classical allusion in *Paradise Lost* that shaped my own understanding of the essential violence of Milton's allusive appropriations, see Gordon Teskey, "A Bleeding Rib: Milton and Classical Culture," in *Delirious Milton: The Fate of the Poet in Modernity* (Cambridge, MA: Harvard UP, 2006), 107–128.

15 See Teskey, "On the Origin in *Paradise Lost*," in *The Poetry of John Milton* (Cambridge, MA: Harvard UP, 2015), 340–369.

Works Cited and Consulted

Abbate, Carolyn. *Unsung Voices: Opera and Musical Narrative in the Nineteenth Century*. Princeton, NJ: Princeton UP, 1991.

Achinstein, Sharon. "*Samson Agonistes.*" *A Companion to Milton*. Edited by Thomas N. Corns. Oxford: Blackwell, 2003. 411–428.

Ainsworth, David. *Milton, Music and Literary Interpretation: Reading through the Spirit*. New York: Routledge, 2020.

Ainsworth, David. "Rapturous Milton and the Communal Harmony of Faith." *Milton Quarterly* 47.3 (2013): 149–62.

Akopyan, Ovanes. "Sing Aloud Harmonious Spheres: Renaissance Conceptions of Cosmic Harmony*, by Jacomien Prins and Maude Vanhaelen (eds.).*" Book review. *Nuncius: Journal of the Material and Visual History of Science* 34.2 (2019): 463–464.

Albright, Daniel. *Musicking Shakespeare: A Conflict of Theatres*. Eastman Studies in Music. Rochester, NY: U Rochester P, 2007.

Altegoer, Diana B. "*Milton among the Philosophers* (Fallon); and *Contemplation of Created Things* (Marjara)." Book review. *Configurations* 3.3 (1995): 441–444.

Barclay, Bill and David Lindley, eds. *Shakespeare, Music and Performance*. Cambridge, UK: Cambridge UP, 2017.

Basile, Mary Elizabeth. "The Music of *A Maske.*" *Milton Quarterly* 27.3 (Oct. 1993): 85–98.

Bennett, Joan S. "A Reading of *Samson Agonistes.*" *The Cambridge Companion to Milton*. Edited by Dennis Danielson. Cambridge, UK: Cambridge UP, 1989, 225–241.

Berley, Marc. *After the Heavenly Tune: English Poetry and the Aspiration to Song*. Pittsburgh, PA: Duquesne UP, 2000.

Bloom, Gina. *Voice in Motion: Staging Gender, Shaping Sound in Early Modern England*. Philadelphia: U Pennsylvania P, 2007.

Boesky, Amy. "Milton's Heaven and the Model of the English Utopia." *Studies in English Literature, 1500–1900* 36.1, The English Renaissance (Winter, 1996): 91–110.

Bribitzer-Stull, Matthew. *Understanding the Leitmotif: From Wagner to Hollywood Film Music*. Cambridge, UK: Cambridge UP, 2015.

Bridges, Robert. *Milton's Prosody, with a Chapter on Accentual Verse & Notes*. 2nd edition. Oxford, UK: Oxford UP, 1921.
Brophy, James D. "Milton's 'Warble': The Trill as Metaphor of Concord." *Milton Quarterly* 19.4 (Dec. 1985): 105–109.
Buhler, Stephen M. "Counterpoint and Controversy: Milton and the Critiques of Polyphonic Music." *Milton Studies* 36 (1998): 18–40.
Buhler, Stephen M. "'Soft *Lydian* Airs' Meet 'Anthems clear': Intelligibility in Milton, Handel, and Mark Morris." *John Donne Journal* 25 (2006): 333–353.
Burnett, Archie. "Introduction." *A Variorum Commentary on the Poems of John Milton. Volume 3:* Samson Agonistes, by Stephen B. Dobranski. Pittsburgh, PA: Duquesne UP, 2009. 1–46.
Carey, John. "A Work in Praise of Terrorism? September 11 and *Samson Agonistes*." *TLS* (6 Sept. 2002): 15–16.
Carpenter, Nan Cooke. "Milton and Music: Henry Lawes, Dante, and Casella." *English Literary Renaissance* 2.2 (Spring 1972): 237–242.
Cavalieri, Emilio de. *Rappresentatione di Anima, et di Corpo*. Liner notes. Performed by M.C. Chappuis et al., Staatsopernchor Berlin, and Akademie für Alte Musik Berlin. Conducted by René Jacobs. harmonia mundi, 2015. CD and MP3.
Chłopicka, Regina. "*Paradise Lost*: A Contemporary Interpretation of the Biblical Story of Salvation." *Krzysztof Penderecki's Music in the Context of 20th-Century Theatre*. Edited by Teresa Malecka. Kraków: Akademia Muzyczna, 1999. 141–148.
Cox, Katherine. "'How cam'st thou speakable of mute': Satanic Acoustics in *Paradise Lost*." *Milton Studies* 57 (2016): 233–260.
Creaser, John. "'Fear of Change': Closed Minds and Open Forms in Milton." *Milton Quarterly* 42.3 (Oct. 2008): 161–182.
Creaser, John. "The Line in *Paradise Lost*." *The Cambridge Companion to Paradise Lost*. Edited by Louis Schwartz. Cambridge: Cambridge UP, 2014. 81–93.
Creaser, John. "'Service Is Perfect Freedom': Paradox and Prosodic Style in *Paradise Lost*." *The Review of English Studies*, New series 58.235 (June 2007): 268–315.
Davidson, Audrey. "Milton on the Music of Henry Lawes." *Milton Newsletter* 2.2 (May 1968): 19–23.
Delloff, Linda Marie. "A Fall From Grace." *Christian Century* 96.2 (Jan. 17, 1979): 52–54.
Dobranski, Stephen B. *A Variorum Commentary on the Poems of John Milton. Volume 3:* Samson Agonistes. Pittsburgh, PA: Duquesne UP, 2009.
Draus, Agnieszka. "Krzysztof Penderecki, *Paradise Lost*. From Milton's Poem to the *sacra rappresentazione* Libretto." Translated by Jan Rybicki. *Krzysztof Penderecki's Music in the Context of 20th-Century Theatre*. Edited by Teresa Malecka. Kraków: Akademia Muzyczna, 1999. 173–179.
Duerden, Rachel. "The Mis-shapen Pearl: Morris, Handel, Milton, and *L'Allegro, il Penseroso ed il Moderato*." *Dance Research: The Journal for the Society for Dance Research* 28.2 (Nov. 2010): 200–217.

Works Cited and Consulted 131

Dunn, Leslie C., and Katherine R. Larson, eds. *Gender and Song in Early Modern England*. Farnham/Burlington: Ashgate, 2014.

Eliot, T. S. "Milton I" and "Milton II." *On Poetry and Poets*. New York: Farrar, Straus and Giroux, 2009 (1957). 156–164, 165–183.

Fallon, Stephen. "The Metaphysics of Milton's Divorce Tracts." *Politics, Poetics, and Hermeneutics in Milton's Prose*. Edited by David A. Loewenstein and James Grantham Turner. Cambridge, UK: Cambridge University Press, 1990. 69–83.

Fallon, Stephen. *Milton among the Philosophers*. Ithaca, NY: Cornell UP, 1991.

Fish, Stanley Eugene. *Surprised by Sin: The Reader in* Paradise Lost. Berkeley and Los Angeles: U California P, 1971.

Fish, Stanley Eugene. "'There Is Nothing He Cannot Ask': Milton, Liberalism, and Terrorism." *Versions of Antihumanism: Milton and Others*. Cambridge: Cambridge UP, 2012. 79–97.

Fry, Christopher. Libretto. *Paradise Lost*. Music by Krzysztof Penderecki. Original text by John Milton. Mainz, Germany: Schott Music GmbH & Co. KG, 1978.

Gregory, Tobias. "The Political Messages of *Samson Agonistes*." *Studies in English Literature 1500–1900* 50.1 (Winter 2010): 175–203.

Haar, James. "Review: *Musical Backgrounds for English Literature: 1580–1650* by Gretchen Ludke Finney." *Journal of the American Musicological Society* 17.2 (Summer 1964): 214–218.

Hamilton, Newburgh. Libretto. *Samson*. Music by George Frideric Handel. Edited by Friedrich Chrysander. *Georg Friedrich Händels Werke*. Band 10. Leipzig: Deutsche Händelgesellschaft, 1861.

Hamilton, Newburgh. Libretto. *Samson*. Music by George Frideric Handel. Performed by the Sixteen and the Symphony of Harmony and Invention. Conducted by Harry Christophers. Coro, 2002. CD and MP3.

Handel, George Frideric. *L'Allegro, il Pensieroso, ed il Moderato*. 1740. Edited by Friedrich Chrysander. *Georg Friedrich Händels Werke*. Band 6. Leipzig: Deutsche Händelgesellschaft, 1859.

Handel, George Frideric. *L'Allegro, il Penseroso, ed il Moderato*. Performed by Gabrieli Consort and Players. Conducted by Paul McCreesh. Signum Classics, 2015. CD and MP3.

Handel, George Frideric. *Samson*. 1743. Edited by Friedrich Chrysander. *Georg Friedrich Händels Werke*. Band 10. Leipzig: Deutsche Händelgesellschaft, 1861.

Handel, George Frideric. *Samson*. Performed by the Sixteen and the Symphony of Harmony and Invention. Conducted by Harry Christophers. Coro, 2002. CD and MP3.

Harper, David A. "The First Annotator of *Paradise Lost* and the Makings of English Literary Criticism." *Studies in English Literature 1500–1900* 59.3 (Summer 2019): 507–530.

Harper, John. "'One Equal Music': The Music of Milton's Youth." *Milton Quarterly* 31.1 (Mar. 1997): 1–10.

Harris, Ellen T. *George Frideric Handel: A Life with Friends*. New York: W.W. Norton & Company, 2014.

Harris, James and Charles Jennens. Libretto. *L'Allegro, il Penseroso, ed il Moderato*. Music by George Frideric Handel. Performed by Gabrieli Consort and Players. Conducted by Paul McCreesh. Signum Classics, 2015. CD and MP3.

Harris, James and Charles Jennens. Libretto. *L'Allegro, il Penseroso, ed il Moderato*. Music by George Frideric Handel. 1740. Edited by Friedrich Chrysander. *Georg Friedrich Händels Werke*. Band 6. Leipzig: Deutsche Händelgesellschaft, 1859.

Hicks, Anthony. "G.F. Handel (1685–1759): Samson." Liner notes. *Samson*. Performed by the Sixteen and the Symphony of Harmony and Invention. Conducted by Harry Christophers. Coro, 2002. CD and MP3.

Hollander, John. *The Untuning of the Sky: Ideas of Music in English Poetry 1500–1700*. Princeton: Princeton University Press, 1961.

Kelley, Maurice. Introduction and notes to *Christian Doctrine*. *Complete Prose Works of John Milton, Vol. 6: Christian Doctrine*. New Haven: Yale University Press, 1973. 3–116.

Knoppers, Laura Lunger. "Headnote: i. Dating." *The Complete Works of John Milton, Volume 2: The 1671 Poems: Paradise Regained and Samson Agonistes*. Edited by Laura Lunger Knoppers. Oxford: Oxford University Press, 2008. lxxxviii–xcviii.

Lange, Art. "Penderecki's 'Paradise Lost.'" *Tempo* New series 128 (Mar. 1979): 34–5.

Larson, Katherine R. "'Blest pair of *Sirens*... Voice and Verse': Milton's Rhetoric of Song." *Milton Studies* 54 (2013): 81–106.

Larson, Katherine R. *The Matter of Song in Early Modern England: Texts in and of the Air*. Oxford, UK: Oxford UP, 2019.

Lawes, Henry. *Comus*. Directed by George Rylands. Sound recording. London: Argo, 1968.

Lawes, Henry. *The Masque of Comus*. Edited by Frederick Bridge. Musical score. London: Novello and Company, 1956.

Leaver, Robin A. "Suggestions for Future Research into Bach and the Chorale: Aspects of Repertoire, Pedagogy, Theory and Practice." *Bach* 42.2 (2011): 40–63.

Leonard, John. *Faithful Labourers: A Reception History of Paradise Lost, 1667–1970*. In two volumes. Oxford, UK: Oxford UP, 2013.

Lewalski, Barbara Kiefer. *Milton's Brief Epic: The Genre, Meaning, and Art of Paradise Regained*. Providence: Brown UP, 1966.

Lewalski, Barbara Kiefer. *The Life of John Milton*. Revised edition. Oxford: Blackwell, 2003.

Loewenstein, David. "*Samson Agonistes* and the Culture of Religious Terror." *Milton in the Age of Fish: Essays on Authorship, Text, and Terrorism*. Edited by Michael Lieb and Albert C. Labriola. Pittsburgh: Duquesne UP, 2006. 203–228.

Mander, M. N. K. "Milton and the Music of the Spheres." *Milton Quarterly* 24.2 (May 1990): 63–71.

Mander, M. N. K. "Music in Milton's *Hymn*." *Renaissance Studies* 5.4 (Dec. 1991): 412–426.

Mander, M. N. K. "The *Epistola ad Patrem*: Milton's Apology for Poetry." *Milton Quarterly* 23.4 (Dec. 1989): 158–166.

Marcus, Leah. "John Milton's *Comus*." *A Companion to Milton*. Edited by Thomas N. Corns. Oxford, UK: Blackwell, 2001. 232–245.

Marjara, Harinder S. "Milton's 'Chromatick jarres' and 'Tuscan Aire.'" *Milton Quarterly* 19.1 (Mar. 1985): 11–13.

Marlowe, Christopher. *Doctor Faustus*. *Christopher Marlowe: The Complete Plays*. Edited by Frank Romany and Robert Lindsey. London: Penguin Books, 2003. 341–395.

Mattison, Andrew. "Sweet Imperfection: Milton and the Troubled Metaphor of Harmony." *Modern Philology* 106.4 (May 2009): 617–647.

McColley, Diane Kelsey. *Poetry and Music in Seventeenth-Century England*. Cambridge, England: Cambridge UP, 1997.

Milton, John. *Christian Doctrine*. *Complete Prose Works of John Milton, Vol. 6: Christian Doctrine*. Translated by John Carey. Edited by Maurice Kelley. General editor Don M. Wolfe. New Haven: Yale UP, 1973.

Milton, John. *John Milton: The Complete Poems*. Edited by John Leonard. London, UK: Penguin, 2007.

Milton, John. *The Complete Poetry and Essential Prose of John Milton*. Edited by William Kerrigan, John Rumrich, and Stephen M. Fallon. New York: Random House, 2007.

Milton, John. *Milton: The Complete Shorter Poems*. Edited by John Carey. Revised 2nd edition. Harlow, UK: Longman, 2007.

Milton, John. *The Complete Works of John Milton, Volume 2: The 1671 Poems: Paradise Regained and Samson Agonistes*. Edited by Laura Lunger Knoppers. Oxford: Oxford UP, 2008.

Milton, John. "Of Education." *Complete Prose Works of John Milton, Volume 2*. Edited by Ernest Sirluck. General editor Don M. Wolfe. New Haven: Yale UP, 1959.

Milton, John. *Paradise Lost*. Edited by Alastair Fowler. Revised 2nd edition. Harlow, UK: Longman, 2007.

Milton, John. *Paradise Lost*. Edited by Barbara K. Lewalski. Oxford: Blackwell Publishing, 2007.

Milton, John. *Paradise Lost*. Edited by Gordon Teskey. Norton Critical Edition. 1st edition. New York: W. W. Norton & Company, 2005.

Minear, Erin. *Reverberating Song in Shakespeare and Milton: Language, Memory, and Musical Representation*. Burlington, VT: Ashgate, 2011.

Minear, Erin. "Review: *Voice in Motion: Staging Gender, Shaping Sound in Early Modern England* by Gina Bloom." *Early Modern Women* 3 (Fall 2008): 333–335.

Mohamed, Feisal G. "Confronting Religious Violence: Milton's *Samson Agonistes*." *PMLA* 120.2 (Mar. 2005): 327–340.

Morris, Brian. "'Not Without Song': Milton and the Composers." *Approaches to Paradise Lost*. Edited by C.A. Patrides. London: Edward Arnold, 1968. 137–161.

Mueller, Janel. "Just Measures? Versification in *Samson Agonistes*." *Milton Studies* 33, The Miltonic Samson (1996): 47–82.
Murphy, Scott. "In the Beginning of Penderecki's *Paradise Lost*." *Twentieth-Century Music* 10.2 (Sept. 2013): 231–248.
O'Connell, Michael and John Powell. "Music and Sense in Handel's Setting of Milton's *L'Allegro* and *Il Penseroso*." *Eighteenth-Century Studies* 12.1 (Autumn 1978): 16–46.
Oxford English Dictionary. *OED Online*. Oxford UP, Dec. 2022. www.oed.com.
Pecheux, Mother M. Christopher. "'At a Solemn Musick': Structure and Meaning." *Studies in Philology* 75.3 (Summer 1978): 331–346.
Penderecki, Krzysztof. *Paradise Lost*. Musical score. Libretto by Christopher Fry. Original text by John Milton. Mainz, Germany: Schott Music GmbH & Co. KG, 1978.
Penderecki, Krzysztof. *Paradise Lost*. Performed by Lyric Opera of Chicago. Conducted by Bruno Bartoletti. 29 Nov. 1978. As posted on youtube.com 24 Feb. 2011. Accessed 2 Mar. 2023. In four parts:
Act 1, Part 1: https://youtu.be/_Z75cdL2Kv8
Act 1, Part 2: https://youtu.be/4PiJi8Krkp4
Act 2, Part 1: https://youtu.be/MBv8qXMSwBQ
Act 2, Part 2: https://youtu.be/2DD4IhFFDTo
Porter, Andrew. "Theme Sublime." *Musical Events*. *The New Yorker*. Dec. 18, 1978 (Vol. 54): 88, 90, 95, 98, 103 (5 pp. discontinuously printed).
Prince, F.T. *The Italian Element in Milton's Verse*. Oxford: Clarendon Press, 1954.
Prins, Jacomien, and Maude Vanhaelen, eds. *Sing Aloud Harmonious Spheres: Renaissance Conceptions of Cosmic Harmony*. New York/London: Routledge, 2018.
Radzinowicz, Mary Ann. *Towards "Samson Agonistes": The Growth of Milton's Mind*. Princeton, NJ: Princeton UP, 1978.
Rajan, B. "Milton and Eliot: A Twentieth-Century Acknowledgment." *Milton Studies* 11, The Presence of Milton (1978): 115–129.
Revard, Stella P. "Handel's *Samson:* London, 1985," *Milton Quarterly* 21.1 (Mar. 1987): 28–30.
Robinson, Ray. "Some Problems of Instrumentation in Penderecki's Opera *Paradise Lost* (1975–78)." *Krzysztof Penderecki's Music in the Context of 20th-Century Theatre*. Edited by Teresa Malecka. Kraków: Akademia Muzyczna, 1999. 149–160.
Rogers, John. *The Matter of Revolution: Science, Poetry, and Politics in the Age of Milton*. Ithaca, NY: Cornell UP, 1996.
Rumrich, John Peter. *Matter of Glory: A New Preface to* Paradise Lost. Pittsburgh: U Pittsburgh P, 1987.
Saal, Hubert. "Trouble in Paradise." *Newsweek* Dec. 11, 1978 (Vol. 92): 90.
Sherry, Beverley. "Milton, Materialism, and the Sound of *Paradise Lost*." *Essays in Criticism* 60.3 (July 2010): 220–241.

Shuger, Debora. "Portrait of the Artist as a Young? (or Milton's Religion: The Early Years)." Tenth International Milton Symposium. Aoyama Gakuin University. Tokyo, Japan. Aug. 23, 2012. Plenary lecture. Lecture published online at http://ims10.blogspot.jp/2009/08/portrait-of-artist-as-young.html. Accessed 2 March 2023.

Smith, Ruth. "Milton Modulated for Handel's Music." *Milton in the Long Restoration*. Edited by Blair Hoxby and Ann Baynes Coiro. Oxford, UK: Oxford UP, 2016. 159–177.

Smith, Ruth. "'Something of a Gayer Turn': Why Handel Laid Aside Messiah in 1740." Liner notes. Performed by Gabrieli Consort and Players. Conducted by Paul McCreesh. Signum Records, 2015. CD and MP3.

Spitzer, Leo. "Classical and Christian Ideas of World Harmony: Prolegomena to an Interpretation of the Word 'Stimmung' (Part II)." *Traditio* 3 (1945): 307–364.

Stanwood, Paul G. "'Paradise Lost': Epic and Opera." *Early Modern Literary Studies* 15.3 (Jan. 2011). Web. Accessed 26 Apr. 2015. https://extra.shu.ac.uk/emls/15-3/stanpl2.htm.

Sugimura, N. K. *"Matter of Glorious Trial": Spiritual and Material Substance in Paradise Lost*. New Haven, CT: Yale UP, 2009.

Teskey, Gordon. *Delirious Milton: The Fate of the Poet in Modernity*. Cambridge, MA: Harvard UP, 2006.

Teskey, Gordon. "On the Origin in *Paradise Lost*." *The Poetry of John Milton*. Cambridge, MA: Harvard UP, 2015. 340–369.

Tillyard, E. M. W. *Milton*. Revised edition with a preface by Phyllis B. Tillyard. New York: Collier Books, 1967.

Waddington, Raymond B. "A Musical Source for *L'Allegro*?" *Milton Quarterly* 27.2 (May 1993): 72–74.

Wójtowicz, Ewa. "Some Harmonic Aspects of Krzysztof Penderecki's *Paradise Lost*." *Krzysztof Penderecki's Music in the Context of 20th-Century Theatre*. Edited by Teresa Malecka. Kraków: Akademia Muzyczna, 1999. 161–171.

Wright, George T. *Shakespeare's Metrical Art*. Berkeley and Los Angeles: U California P, 1988.

Wright, Thomas. *The Passions of the Minde in Generall. Corrected, enlarged, and with sundry new discourses augmented*. London, 1604. *Early English Books Online*. http://name.umdl.umich.edu/A15775.0001.001. Accessed 2 March 2023.

Yeats, William Butler. *The Collected Poems of W.B. Yeats*. Edited by Richard J. Finneran. Revised 2nd edition. New York: Scribner Paperback Poetry, 1996.

Index

Note: Page numbers in **bold** indicate tables on the corresponding pages. Endnotes are indicated by the page number followed by "n" and the note number e.g., 10n3 refers to note 3 on page 10.

Adam: in *Paradise Lost* (Milton) 21–23, 24–25, 27, 28, 35, 43–44, 45, 50, 60–61n9, 92, 99, 102, 111n3; in *Paradise Lost* (Penderecki) 91–92, **93–94**, 95–98, 99–103, 107, 110, 111n3, 112n10, 112n13, 125; *see also* Eve
Addison, Joseph 123
Ainsworth, David 2, 11n8, 11n9, 11n15, 35n12, 42, 60n7, 61n14, 87n2, 110n1, 128n12, 128n13
Albright, Daniel 12n17
allegory 31, 37n26, 37n27, 118, 119–120
angelic music 21–24, 40, 45–46, 48–50, 61n10, 61n11, 61n13, 62–63n16, 63n23, 93–94
animist materialism 19, 20, 22, 25, 31, 32, 34n5, 35n8; *see also* monist materialism
Areopagitica 34n7, 124
Aristotle 5, 11n14, 20–21
"At a Solemn Music" 6, 27–29, 31, 32, 36n21, 37n24, 38–42, 45, 56, 58, 59n1, 59n3, 59n4, 60n6, 60n9, 63n24, 85, 90n22, 99, 114n21, 115, 116, 119, 120, 122, 126, 126n2

Bach, J. S. 76, 108, 109, 125, 112n11, 114n23, 125; *see also St. John Passion*
Berley, Marc 2, 10n3

Bloom, Gina 17, 33n2
Buhler, Stephen 2, 10n4, 12n18, 36n14, 62n16

cacophony 8, 56–58, 67–73, 78, 83–4, 86–87, 92, 98, 119, 123–124
Carey, John 36n19, 36n21, 59n1, 60n6, 89n12, 116, 117, 124, 128n10
charm, charming 45, 47, 48, 49–50, 53
Chłopicka, Regina 92, 97, 111n6, 111n7, 112n10, 112–113n14, 114n21
Christian Doctrine, The or *De Doctrina Christiana* 5, 19, 32–33
concent 27, 39, 42, 59n1, 59n2, 59n3
concord 45–46, 48, 104
consort 26, 32, 41–42
Cox, Katherine 2, 10n6, 35n8
Cowper, William 123

Dagon 67, 68, 69, 71–72, 77, 80–82, 83–84, 90n21
dissonance 53, 56, 62n16, 63n24, 91–92, 97–98
Dickinson, Emily 120
Draus, Agnieszka 111n4, 111n6, 111n7, 111n17
Dryden, John 120

Eve: in *Paradise Lost* (Milton) 21, 24–25, 43–44, 50, 60–61n9, 92, 99, 102, 111n3; in *Paradise Lost*

Index 137

(Penderecki) 91–93, **93–94**, 95–98, 99–103, 107, 110, 111n3, 112n10, 112n13, 125; *see also* Adam

Fall, the 9, 24, 29, 32, 49–50, 91–93, **93–94**, 95, 98–99, 103, 107, 110, 111n3, 125
Fallon, Stephen 5, 19, 20–21, 27, 31, 33
false relation (in music) 98, 102–103, 113n15
Fish, Stanley 125, 128n10, 128n11
Fry, Christopher 93, 99, 102

God (God the Father): body of 17, 20, 33n1, 36n15; creation of matter by 24; Hebrew God 82, 85, 124; in Milton's works 3, 6, 18–19, 21–22, 23, 24–25, 28–29, 32, 38–46, **48**, 49–50, 61n11, 63n23, 95, 114n24, 115, 119, 120, 122–126; in *Paradise Lost* (Penderecki) **94**, 95, 98, 100, 107, 111n6; music expressing praise of and obedience to 21, 24–25, 43–46, 58, 109

Hamilton, Newburgh 37n24, 71, 76–77, 78–79, 82–83, 85–86, 88n5, 89n19
Handel, G. F. 8, 11–12n16, 12n18, 12n19, 37n24, 67–68, 71–87, 88n5, 88n6, 88n7, 88n10, 88n11, 89n14, 89n15, 89n16, 89n17, 89n18, 90n21, 90n22, 92, 98, 115–124, 126, 126–127n2; contrast with Milton's cacophony 85–87; *see also L'Allegro, il Penseroso, ed il Moderato and Samson*
harmony 3, 4, 8, 23, 39–40, 42, 44, 45–46, 59n3, 61n12, 61n14, 62–63n16, 63n24, 100, 102, 109, 112–113n14, 116, 117, 119; of the spheres 17, 26–27, 33n3; tonal harmony 63n24, 71, 87, 109–110; post-tonal harmony 8, 67, 87, 92, 97–99, 109; *see also* concord, dissonance, false relation
Harper, David A. 12n20, 128n9
Harris, Ellen T. 84–85, 88n10, 90n21, 124
Harris, James 116, 127n3

Haydn, Franz Joseph 7
Hayes, Terrance 120
heavenly music vs. infernal music 47–50, **48**
Herbert, George 120
Hollander, John 46–47, 49, 50, 59n3
Hughes, Langston 120
Hume, Peter 12n20, 123, 128n9

Il Penseroso (Milton) 11n16, 12n18, 34n6, 115, 121, 127–128n7
infernal music 23–24, 36n14, 46–51, **48**, 62–63n16

Jennens, Charles 116–117, 126–127n2, 127n3
Johnson, Samuel 123

L'Allegro (Milton) 11–12n16, 115–123, 127n4, 127–128n7
L'Allegro, il Penseroso, ed il Moderato (Handel) 12n18, 86, 88n10, 90n22, 115, 116–122, 123
Larson, Katherine R. 2, 10n5, 33n2
Lawes, Henry 11n16, 53
Leonard, John 111n3
Lewalski, Barbara Kiefer 34n5, 35n8, 37n26
Lyric Opera of Chicago 9, 112n9

Manoa: in *Samson* (Handel) 71–77, 83, 88n6; in *Samson Agonistes* (Milton), 56–57, 68–69, 70
Masque presented at Ludlow Castle, 1634, A 6, 10n1, 34n6, 34–35n7, 37n26, 29–32, 51–55, 56, 58, 63n17, 63n18, 63n19, 63n20, 63n21, 82, 87, 115, 121, 126, 127n7
Marcus, Leah 63n21
Mattison, Andrew 2, 10n3
McColley, Diane Kelsey 3, 11n10, 59n4, 62n16
melisma 73, 116–118
Messias **94**, 107–110, 111n5
meter (in poetry) 37n26, 53, 69–70, 87n2, 88n4
Michael **94**, 103, 105, 109–110
Minear, Erin 2, 10–11n7, 50–51, 60n6, 60n7, 60–61n9, 63n18, 63n19, 60n20

Index

monist materialism 5–6, 18–23, 25, 27–28, 31–33, 34n4, 34n5, 34–35n7, 34n8, 38, 68, 70, 87, 122; *see also* animist materialism
Murphy, Scott 112–113n14

"Ode on the Morning of Christ's Nativity" 6, 19, 25–27, 28, 30, 34n6, 36n19, 36n20, 36n21
"Of Education" 3–5, 20, 28

Paradise Lost (Milton) 2, 5, 6, 8–9, 12n20, 17, 19, 20, 21–25, 26–27, 28, 29, 31, 35n8, 35n12, 39, 42–51, 52, 54, 55, 56, 58, 60n7, 60–61n9, 61n11, 62–63n17, 70, 87, 87n3, 92, 99, 102, 104, 110, 110n1, 111n3, 111n5, 115, 124–125; Adam and Eve's production of sound in 24–25, 43–44; agency of music in 21–22, 27, 29; angelic music in 21–24; meter in 70; Milton's representation of music in 17, 19–20; monist music in 20–22; music as sound and metaphor in 42–46, 54–55, 58; infernal music in 23–24, 46–49
Paradise Lost (Penderecki) 8–9, 13n21, 87, 91–110, 124–126; Adam and Eve's departure from Paradise in 99–100; Adam and Eve's duet in 95–98; climax of 108–109; "Concourse in arms" chorus in 103–104, 107–108; "Dies irae" chorus in 104–106; dissonance in 91–92, 97–98; Messias's decision to sacrifice himself in 110; plot sequence of 92–93, **93–94**; prelapsarian world and marriage of Adam and Eve in 100–102; sound of fallenness in 98–99, 102–103, 109–110
Paradise Regained 19, 20, 32, 56, 63n23, 113n17
Passions of the Mind, The 11n14, 17–19, 34n4
Penderecki, Krzysztof 8–9, 13n21, 87, 91–110, 110n1, 111n2–7, 112n12–14, 112n9–10, 113n15–19, 114n24–25, 114n21–22, 115, 124–126, 128n12–13; *see also Paradise Lost* (Penderecki), *Threnody for the Victims of Hiroshima*
Plato 4, 5, 11n14, 20–21, 34–35n7, 127n4; *see also Republic, The*
Pope, Alexander 123
Porter, Andrew 13n21, 113n15, 113n17, 114n22, 114n25
postlapsarian music (or fallen music): in Milton's works 23–24, 26–29, 36n14, 38, 41, 46–50, 51–55, 62–63n16; in *Paradise Lost* (Penderecki) 9, 92–93, 95–99, 99–107, 125
prelapsarian music: in Milton's works 20–22, 23, 29–30, 32, 36n14, 41, 42–43, 50–51, 60–61n9, 62–63n16, 87; in *Paradise Lost* (Penderecki) 100–102, 125

Raphael 21, 22, 35n11, 35n12, **94**, 95
Republic, The 4, 127n4
Robinson, Ray 111n6, 113n16
Rogers, John 34–35n7
Rumrich, John 34–35n7, 62n16

Sacra Rappresentazione 9, 111n4, 113n15
Samson: in *Samson* (Handel) 71, 74, 76, 79, 80, 83–85, 87, 89n15, 90n21; in *Samson Agonistes* (Milton) 8, 55–58, 67–68, 70, 78–79, 87, 124, 125, 128n10
Samson (Handel) 8, 12n18, 37n24, 67–68, 71–87; Chorus of the Philistines in 79–82, 123–124; Hebrew Chorus in 82–83; Israelite woman's song in 84–85; cacophony as loss of musical voice in 83–84, 86–87
Samson Agonistes (Milton) 6, 8, 19, 55–58, 115–119, 123, 124–125; meter in 69–70; cacophony in 56–58, 67–70
Satan 2, 50, 63n23, 92, 93, **93–94**, 95, 97, 100, 102, 111n6, 112n10, 112–113n14, 113n17
Schoenberg, Arnold 67

Shakespeare, William 7, 10–11n7, 12n17, 33n2, 50–51, 88n4, 120
Sherry, Beverley 35n8
Smith, Ruth 12n18, 88n10, 88n11, 89n14, 89n15, 89n19, 90n22, 126–127n2
Son of God, the (also Jesus) 24, 45, 63n23, 94, 95, 111n5, 114n25; *see also Messias*
St. John Passion 109
Stanwood, P. G. 92, 93
stile concitato 97, 112n10
Sugimura, N.K. 34–35n7
suspension (in music) 35–36n13, 49, 61n15

Stravinsky, Igor 67
synesthesia 26, 30, 52

Teskey, Gordon 33n1, 36n15, 55, 61n13, 126, 128n14, 128n15
Threnody for the Victims of Hiroshima 9

wave-particle theory of light 42
Wright, Thomas 11n14, 17–20, 22, 34n4, 123; *see also Passions of the Mind, The*

Yeats, W.B. 120, 121, 128n8

For Product Safety Concerns and Information please contact our EU representative GPSR@taylorandfrancis.com
Taylor & Francis Verlag GmbH, Kaufingerstraße 24, 80331 München, Germany

www.ingramcontent.com/pod-product-compliance
Lightning Source LLC
Chambersburg PA
CBHW051750230426
43670CB00012B/2232